Middle Childhood

of related interest

Child Welfare Services Developments in Law, Policy, Practice and Research
Edited by Malcolm Hill and Jane Aldgate
ISBN 185302 316 7

Social Work with Children and Families
Getting into Practice
Ian Butler and Gwenda Roberts
ISBN 185302 365 5

How We Feel
An Insight into the Emotional World of Teenagers
Edited by Jacki Gordon and Gillian Grant
ISBN 185302 439 2

Middle Childhood

The Perspectives of Children and Parents

Moira Borland, Ann Laybourn,
Malcolm Hill and Jane Brown

Jessica Kingsley Publishers
London and Philadelphia

First published in the United Kingdom in 1998
by Jessica Kingsley Publishers Ltd,
116 Pentonville Road,
London N1 9JB, England
and
325 Chestnut Street, Philadelphia,
PA 19106, USA.

Copyright 1998 Moira Borland, Ann Laybourn,
Malcolm Hill and Jane Brown

Library of Congress Cataloging in Publication Data
A CIP catalogue record for this book is available from the Library of Congress

British Library Cataloguing in Publication Data
Middle Childhood
I.Borland, Moira
305.2'34

ISBN 1 85302 472 4 hb
ISBN 1 85302 473 2 pb

Printed and Bound in Great Britain by
Athenaeum Press, Gateshead, Tyne and Wear

CONTENTS

Acknowledgements

We would like to express our appreciation to all the children and parents who talked to us about their views and experiences. We are grateful to the Health Education Board for Scotland which funded the two studies on which the book is based. Jenny Secker, Kathryn Milburn and members of the advisory groups gave us great support and encouragement.

Note

This book makes considerable use of quotations. These were transcribed verbatim from tape-recordings of interviews and group discussions. When a change of speaker occurred in a group discussion this is indicated with a — in the text. Very occasionally irrelevant material is omitted from the quote, which is indicated thus: (...).

CHAPTER 1

Introduction

Many books are available about young children and parenting in the early years before school starts. Likewise, much has been written about teenagers and their families. The in-between period is relatively neglected. Very few popular or academic writings have focused on the needs, development and experiences of primary school-aged children and their families.

With this volume we are hoping to begin to fill that gap in relation to middle childhood. The contents are largely based on views expressed to us by children and parents themselves in two studies carried out for the Health Education Board for Scotland aimed to identify the main issues affecting families at this life stage in Britain today.

The changing context of childhood

'To suggest that children growing up in the 1990s live in a very different world from the one their parents or grandparents experienced as children is not only to state the obvious but to *understate* the obvious' (Murray 1993, p.9). In the Western world economic and technological development has dramatically altered many of the features of daily life for most children.

Cars, televisions and computers were rare and expensive items 50 years ago, but are now commonplace. Most children now walk less and travel further more often. Instant access to news from across the world has contributed to a greater awareness of other peoples and countries. Supermarkets have proliferated and provide a much wider range of foods and goods than was available in the typical shop or store in the 1950s. In an absolute sense most children and their families are materially better off than their parents' generations were, though many families still struggle financially to feed, clothe and generally provide for their children in a society where inequalities have widened in the last two decades (Alcock 1993; Kumar 1993). More children than ever before proceed to higher education and university, but higher proportions also face extended periods of unemployment (Jones and Wallace 1992).

The demography of childhood has changed significantly too. Divorce, lone parenthood and step-parenthood have grown markedly. Children are more likely to have to handle major changes in their household than formerly. Many urban areas in particular now have a considerable ethnic diversity. Medical advances have meant that an increasing number of new-borns with severe disabilities survive and so children and adults with severe disabilities become more numerous.

These and other developments represent the contexts in which children live. It is much harder to assess what this all means for children and their families – though many have opinions. Figures showing increased juvenile crime and drug-taking lead some to bemoan moral degeneration. In some parts of the media, young people are demonised. The large rise in *reported* incidents of child abuse reminds us that too many children are victims.

In one sense it would seem safe to say that children are prominent members of society. Much money and effort is invested in their schooling, even if debate ensues about the best way to enable individuals to fulfil their potential and achieve a fair distribution of opportunities. Recent children's legislation aimed to protect and promote the interest of the most vulnerable children stresses that children's welfare should be paramount in decisions affecting them (Hill and Aldgate 1996). Commercially, children and their parents now constitute a major market sector, ranging from specialist early years shops and 'learning centres' to outlets for pop CDs and trademark clothes and footwear.

Yet is also possible to argue that children are still neglected and subordinate to adults in many ways (Qvortrup *et al.* 1994). Often their lives are tightly organised by adults. They may well have little freedom over their use of time and different kinds of space, as most places in their environments are now formalised and many preserved for adults. The growth in car ownership has made it easier for adults to get about, but has restricted children's opportunity for independent play and mobility, as neighbourhoods become dominated by busy roads (Davis 1995). It is no longer the case that children are expected to be 'seen but not heard', but their opportunities to express views and influence key decisions affecting them remain quite limited (Franklin 1995). Education legislation has largely seen parents as the consumers of the service and conferred very few participatory rights on children (Marshall 1997; Sinclair 1996).

The changing context of parenting

It is a strange paradox that, at the end of a century which has seen immense efforts made towards helping families bring up their children, parents in the First World appear to be as worried about them as ever. In many ways the job of parenting is easier than it has ever been. Immunisation, antibiotics and (in many countries) universal health care have ensured that almost all parents see their offspring making it into adulthood. An array of welfare benefits and provisions have freed most parents from fears of homelessness and starvation. Technical advances such as washing machines, disposable nappies and collapsible buggies have taken much of the hard grind out of childrearing. In most parts of the world, parents would give their right arms to have the worries that occur in the richer West.

Yet this very degree of progress creates its own anxieties. Parents are programmed to worry about children; that is nature's mechanism for ensuring they have maximum chances of survival. Relieved of the immediate need to find food and shelter we become aware of other less pressing concerns. Now that most children's survival and physical health are assured, parents are free to fret about their social and emotional well-being.

In that sphere, they may indeed have cause for concern. The role and context of parenting has changed in many ways over the past fifty years with important consequences for children (Hill and Tisdall 1997). The changing family structures noted above are not necessarily harmful to children but they do put added pressure on parents to compensate for any difficulties they may encounter (Richards 1995).

Other pressures arise from the dramatic changes that have taken place in men's and women's employment patterns. Although the balance of evidence suggests that having both parents in employment does not adversely affect children's development, there have been some recent studies which suggest that in some circumstances it may do. In addition, juggling outside employment with domestic chores and child care imposes a strain on many women. On the other hand, rising male unemployment has resulted in some fathers becoming more involved with their children or even becoming the main carer while the mother is out at work (Moss 1995). The respective roles of mothers and fathers are therefore shifting, though the tradition that mothers play the prime role in childrearing still holds in most families. Increased occupational and geographical mobility has meant that more parents are bringing up children away from the support of their own extended families. Friends and neighbours may compensate, but otherwise individuals and couples can be thrown back to a larger extent on their own resources, both in terms of day-to-day caring, and in deciding how to parent.

At the same time, parents are increasingly wary of allowing their children access to the world outside the home. The desire to keep children safely within the home, rather than playing outside, has been sharpened by the growth in traffic and the high profile given to stranger-danger. Parents feel obliged to chaperone and restrict their children to a far greater extent than they did even 20 years ago (Roberts, Smith and Bryce 1995).

A further pressure on parents has come through the growing emphasis on a 'child centred' approach to parenting. In the post-war era, experts began to recognise a wide range of social and emotional 'needs' which parents should be meeting (e.g. Pringle 1980). More recently, the emphasis has shifted to the notion of children as having independent 'rights' as enshrined, for example in the United Nations Convention on the Rights of the Child and the introduction of recent children's legislation. The state, as represented by central government and the legal system, has always regulated as well as supported family life, but these developments have lent a new edge to the relationship between state and family, as legislation has sought to give a voice to the child. Although the intention is to balance children's right to self-determination with their parents' right to guide and protect them, such moves are seen by many parents (and indeed other adults such as teachers) as undermining their authority over children, and adding to their uncertainty over what the limits of reasonable parenting and discipline are.

Into this well of parental uncertainty and anxiety have poured a flood of 'advice' books, aimed at every age, stage and family type. Their value to parents must be in doubt when one recalls the wild swings in professional advice that have occurred over the past few generations, from the rigid scheduled feeding regimes of the 1930s to the permissive, demand-fed days of the 1960s and 70s (Hardyment 1983). The advice contained within such manuals is usually based on the personal or professional experience of the author, which may or may not be appropriate to other families. What is usually lacking is any reference to what ordinary parents do and find works, or indeed any recognition that what works for one family may not do so for another.

The parental viewpoint has been conveyed in several studies which examined the many factors that influence how parents bring up their children. Early research identified strong class differences in parenting attitudes and styles, as well as many similarities (Newson and Newson 1976). For example, working-class and middle-class parents, though equally loving and warm towards their children and equally concerned for their best interests, promoted these qualities in different ways. More detailed studies of working-class parenting (e.g. Laybourn 1986) suggested that there are good reasons for these differences, which can be seen as appropriate responses to the environment in which children are growing up.

There are also strong cultural influences on parenting. For example, compared with most white British families, parents of Asian backgrounds value more involvement of the extended family in decision making about children, and in some matters expect children to follow their wishes rather than make independent decisions (Modood, Beishon and Vivdee 1996). West African parents too place a high regard in instilling good character, respect for elders and filial obedience (Nsamenang 1992). It is important to remember, though, that even within a single cultural tradition (e.g. Sikhism) variety exists and so crude generalisations should be avoided.

The importance of parents' and children's perspectives

Behind those studies that have explored parental attitudes and practices lies the belief that a vital first step in offering parenting advice is to find out from parents themselves what issues and concerns are important to them, and how they attempt to deal with them. In a number of fields, including medicine and social work, there is an increasing emphasis on what are variously described as lay, consumer or user perspectives. This is a big advance on earlier prescriptions based solely on 'expert' opinion. However, it still leaves out the perspective of the other major players in the parenting game: the children.

There has of course been a long academic tradition of studying children, which has supplied a wealth of information and concepts about them. These have mostly come from developmental and experimental approaches in child psychology, though also from medicine, education and social work. However, children have mainly been seen as 'objects of study', whether as subjects of experiments, or as respondents to questionnaires, the contents of which have been determined in advance by adults, so that even when they are asked their views, the areas open to discussion have already been decided for them. There has until recently been little or no recognition that children have their own perspectives on situations that concern them, and that they often have an understanding of these situations that is far more sophisticated than adults suppose.

In the last few years, however, there have been an increasing number of studies that start from the child's point of view and enlist their help in deciding what the important issues are (e.g. Buckingham 1993; Ennew 1994; Laybourn, Brown and Hill 1996; Mayall 1993). Research which enlists the help of children as active participants needs careful planning. Many of the same considerations apply as to research with adults: the need to establish rapport, to ensure confidentiality, to explain clearly and honestly the purpose of the study, to ask questions clearly. However, researchers also need to make special efforts to adapt their language to the child's cognitive and linguistic level, to make use of materials and settings they are familiar with and enjoy, and to conduct the encounter in a way that makes sense to the child from their own perspective (Garbarino *et al.* 1992).

In line with these developments, this book aims to inform the current debate on the responsibilities and stresses of parenting by listening to what parents and children themselves have to say about them. In presenting this dual perspective we are looking at the experience of parenting both through the eyes of the 'providers' (parents) and through the eyes of the 'consumers' (children). We have found the process of entering their respective worlds both reassuring and unsettling. The parents we spoke to clearly loved and cared for their children and were deeply concerned to do their best for them; the children recognised their parents had their interests at heart, and knew that they were loved. Yet in some respects, parents seemed surprisingly unaware of what children themselves considered they needed from the adults who cared for them. The concerns and priorities of children and parents often differed, and, when this was the case, they showed little understanding of the other's viewpoint. Children appeared unconcerned about some matters that to parents were of first importance. Parents viewed as trivial some of the issues that concerned children most. We hope this book will help each side to understand and respond to the world of the other.

The studies: aims and methods

The two studies on which this book is based were carried out on behalf of the Health Education Board of Scotland (HEBS). We shall refer to them as the Parenting and Well-being studies. They were both focused on middle childhood and in particular on the main concerns, satisfactions and supports of children and parents as seen from their own perspectives. Both studies were small scale, time limited and qualitative in design. It is important to point out at the outset that each study was separately commissioned and designed; they were not intended to form a basis for comparison. Some of the issues covered overlapped, but in addition each had special elements of its own. Nonetheless, after the event it appeared to us that their separate findings were complementary, and that they each threw a new and interesting light on the findings of the other. All the interviews and discussions with children and parents were carried out by the authors. The people who took part in the two studies lived in diverse locations in Central Scotland, ranging from inner-city areas to quite remote villages and hamlets.

The Parenting study

The Parenting study was carried out as part of a HEBS parenting initiative (Borland *et al.* 1996). It was designed to provide information and ideas which could be used as the basis for an advice booklet for parents and professionals. The main aim of the study was to increase understanding of how parents try to promote the health and well-being of children aged between eight and twelve. This was done by talking with parents who had children of that age about what they saw as their responsibilities, what their main concerns were, and how they tried to deal with them. In addition a smaller number of children in the same age group, generally not related to the parents, were asked to talk about the same issues from their own point of view.

The samples of parents and children were drawn largely from four mainstream primary schools based in contrasting areas: two schools in a peripheral housing scheme with high levels of unemployment, one school in a prosperous suburban area and one school in a rural area. A letter from the research team was distributed by the schools to all children in the appropriate year groups to take home to their parents. The letter explained the purpose of the research and asked parents if they would speak to us themselves and/or allow their children to do so. In addition, a smaller sample of parents in particular circumstances (lone, divorced, adoptive and non-custodial parents) was drawn from various community and self-help groups. Parents were approached through staff of these groups and asked if they would take part.

The methods used to make contact with families put the onus on parents to 'opt in' to the study, and the overall response rate was correspondingly low at 1 in 6. Response was particularly poor from schools in the city scheme, and a second school had to be used to bring numbers up. The low response rate means that a considerable degree of self-selection will have taken place, and it seems a reasonable assumption that the parents who agreed to take part will have been those who were more confident, conscientious and interested in the topic of parenting. This must be borne in mind in considering the findings that follow.

In addition, one important special group remains under-represented in the study: that of step-parents. Ideally we would have liked to have talked to a special group of these particular parents, and strenuous efforts were made to recruit them to the sample. However within the time scale of the study this was not achieved and only a few took part in the study.

A total of 75 parents were interviewed; the ratio of mothers to fathers was 2:1. In all 34 children were seen; again with a higher proportion of females. A considerable range of household structures and urban/rural environments were represented. The 'parents' included married couples, single parents, grandparents (as main carers of their grandchildren), step-parents, foster carers and adoptive parents. Most were in their 30s and 40s.

Parents and children were interviewed either in focus groups or individually. Focus groups allow a broad range of topics to be explored with a number of people, and the debate between them can be helpful in sparking off ideas and clarifying understanding (Kitzinger 1994; Morgan 1993). Individual interviews in contrast allow for more detailed and private discussion of personal experiences. The two are therefore complementary. In both cases, the interviewers raised a number of standard key themes with those taking part, but, as always in qualitative research, they encouraged both parents and children to identify and explore other issues that were important to them. The themes raised with parents were:

- views of parenting
- stress and support for parents
- children's needs and rights
- children's well-being and health education.

In addition to these discussions, parents were asked to fill in an optional brief self-completion questionnaire, asking for their views on all four questions and their experience of the group.

Children were asked about a similar set of themes, but to help them feel at ease and to encourage discussion, a variety of techniques and materials were used:

- prompt cards listing what parents should do for children (e.g. love you, feed and care for you, spend time with you)
- brainstorming ideas on the 'ideal' parent
- health promotion images
- asking children to produce drawings of healthy and unhealthy people.

The response from parents was very positive. They spoke about their parenting role with considerable energy and interest. The groups suggested that parents of this age group derive much enjoyment and satisfaction from discussing their role with others. The response from children was more mixed. While some were very forthcoming, a number were more reticent, especially in individual interviews. It may be that the topic of parenting was one which was hard for them to approach directly, since children in the Well-being study had much to say about parenting in the course of considering other topics.

The majority of interviews and group discussions were transcribed. The children's transcripts were analysed by individual questions, the parent transcripts by a coding frame identifying themes as they occurred in the interview.

The children's Well-being study

This separate study was carried out as part of a HEBS initiative to promote children's mental and emotional well-being (Hill, Laybourn and Borland 1995; Hill, Laybourn, Borland and Secker 1996). The aim was to understand how primary age children view and describe their emotional experiences, how other people, including parents, respond to their emotional needs, and how they would like them to respond. It formed the basis for an information leaflet for parents on what they could do to enhance children's emotional well-being and respond to their needs (HEBS 1997).

The study was carried out by talking with children in focus groups and individually. As in the Parenting study, the sample was drawn largely from three mainstream primary schools in contrasting areas; one based in an inner-city area with moderate levels of deprivation and a large ethnic minority population, one in a suburban area, and one in a rural area. In fact, although the suburban area had been selected to give access to a more affluent population, it abutted onto a lower income housing scheme which about half the children in the school came from. It was therefore a more mixed sample than had been intended. In addition, a small sample of children with identified difficulties was drawn from special centres; however, to make a fair comparison with the parents and children in the Parenting study who were all from mainstream schools, we have not considered them in this book.

In this study we used standard consent forms provided by the local authority, accompanied by a letter explaining the research. These forms were distributed to children to take home in the same way as in the Parenting study. In recruiting to the focus groups the forms gave parents the opportunity to opt their children out of the study. However, in recruiting children for individual interviews they had positively to opt them in. Accordingly, response rates were higher for the focus groups than for the individual interviews.

This produced a sample of 69 children between the ages of eight and twelve: 36 girls and 33 boys. (The study in fact also included an additional 59 children aged between four and seven years, but to sharpen comparison with the Parenting study which focused on eight- to eleven-year-olds, they have not generally been considered in this book, except occasionally when it has been helpful to refer to them in order to highlight age differences.) We did not collect details of family background from parents or from children, but it was clear from the children's comments that we had again achieved a fair social mix and different household structures. Most of the children were seen in a total of eight focus groups; a smaller number were interviewed individually.

In view of the wide range of age and ability among the children, we were particularly concerned to make the experience enjoyable and interesting for them. We therefore devised a set of materials to stimulate discussion and capture interest, which were used flexibly according to the age group (Hill, Laybourn and Borland 1996). In the focus groups these included:

- picture cards of different facial expressions for children to interpret
- pictorial vignettes to stimulate ideas on situations evoking emotions
- an imaginary space creature who had no feelings and who asked children to explain what they meant
- brainstorming on various topics
- voting on their relative importance
- direct questioning
- role play.

A similar set of materials was used in the individual interviews, but in addition we used:

- an introductory 'about me' sheet to break the ice and establish that there were no right or wrong answers
- an 'ecomap' or chart of people the child said were important to them
- a set of cards which asked children about their experience of intense emotions (e.g. 'The saddest I've ever been…'), how others had responded, and how they would have liked them to.

As in the parenting study the interviewers raised themes for discussion, but were alert to and encouraged ideas coming spontaneously from the children. At the end of groups and individual interviews, children were asked to:

- fill in a simple self-completion form, asking them about feelings and wishes
- draw a picture of a situation which caused a child to experience a particular feeling.

Most of the children responded with immense enthusiasm and surprising openness to all the topics raised, including the topics of parents as sources of positive and negative emotions and as a source of support. Many children were willing to talk at length about serious personal matters. This was particularly evident in the groups. In individual interviews, the responses were more mixed. Some children seemed inhibited, but others were relaxed and forthcoming, and there were indications that boys particularly found it easier to confide particular fears in a one-to-one situation. This degree of openness must be set in the context that parents could opt their children out of the study; it seems likely that those we saw will have come from families which were more confident and open to outsiders.

Again, all interviews were transcribed, and the results analysed using a combination of methods. Key themes arising in individual and group discussions were identified by careful independent reading by each researcher. Checks were made to find supporting evidence and counter examples for any incipient generalisations. Some of the exercises (such as brainstorming followed by voting) produced standard lists which could be quantified. The self-completion questionnaires also lent themselves to quantification.

Comparing the studies

It will be obvious that contrasts in the purpose and nature of the two studies mean that any apparent similarities and differences between the views of parents and those of children have to be treated with caution. The children and parents in both studies came from a variety of families and areas, so differences between their views could therefore be due to chance. To counteract that possibility, in considering parents' and children's views, we have concentrated on those that arose generally across the sample irrespective of area. In addition we have sought to show how our findings fit with the views of parents and children as represented in other research (see Chapter 11 in particular). Where all these agree, it seems probable, though of course not definite, that the differences found represent real clashes of perspective between parents and children in general.

The book will therefore report the findings of the two studies, providing a double perspective on living through the years of middle childhood. We begin by giving an overview of each perspective; first the parents' viewpoint, then that of the children. Next we move on to look at a number of themes that parents identified as important concerns, and consider how far children agreed with parental definitions of what was 'in the best interests of the child'. In the main part of the book we have aimed to allow the voices of parents and children to come through; to enable them to speak for themselves by using extensive verbatim quotations from the interviews and discussions. At the same time, we have sought to draw out common themes and significant differences in our own commentary.

In order not to interrupt the flow of the text, the main chapters have kept to a minimum references to other sources of information about middle childhood. Chapter 11 provides a review of other academic research and ideas relevant to this period of the life span. The final Chapter 12 identifies key issues arising from our findings in the context of other knowledge and thinking. Implications are discussed for policy, education, service providers and indeed for anyone who has an interest in children and parenting.

We did not want to impose an artificial structure on these views of parents and children which might distort their meaning and importance. This means that there is some unevenness in the various chapters. As would be expected from the distinctive natures of the two studies, we have more material to report from parents about parenting, whilst the children provided more details on aspects of life outside the family – notably their relationships with peer and friends. The comparative sections of the book are not mirrors of each other, but reflect each side's experience of common themes.

This book is aimed at a wide audience. We think it will be of interest to anyone who is interested in parents and children. They will include academics, professionals working with families, parents and, we hope, some children themselves. To make it accessible to such a wide audience, we have tried to keep the style non-technical and 'reader friendly'. We know that, faced with a book of this kind, some people go through it reading only the quotes, others reading everything but them! The research review in Chapter 11 may appear heavy for some; for others it will, we hope, provide an important complement to the perspectives of the people we spoke with. We trust that each kind of reader will find something in the book for them.

CHAPTER 2

The Growing Pains of Middle Childhood

Parents' perspectives on middle childhood

Introduction

It is a truism that expectations and beliefs play a large part in shaping our experience. Two-year-olds and teenagers are meant to be difficult and seldom disappoint us, despite the evidence that, in reality, only a minority are troublesome. There are fewer preconceived notions about how eight- to twelve-year-old children should behave, but in the literature, middle childhood has sometimes been characterised as a lull between the storms and strains of toddlerhood and teens (see Chapter 11). In contrast, the parents we met described it as a turbulent time during which children became increasingly independent, questioning and assertive, while at the same time open to influences from peers and from the media. Whereas the textbooks often suggest that middle childhood is a time when parents can relax somewhat after the practical demands of early childhood and before the emotional demands of dealing with adolescence, the predominant emotion voiced by parents in our study was one of anxiety. This chapter will review broad perceptions of the nature of middle childhood, with specific aspects being followed up in later chapters.

Naturally, parents' perceptions of their children at this stage of life reflected the views they had already formed of children in general and of their own child in particular. They made judgements about competence, vulnerability and susceptibility to negative influences, reflecting classic images of children as either innocent or readily corrupt (Jenks 1996). A child's increasing assertiveness could be seen as broadly positive (independent, capable) or negative (challenging, defiant).

In consequence parents reacted to changes in their children's behaviour in different ways. While some welcomed the increased opportunities for communication and negotiation, others described an on-going battle as parents sought to assert or retain control (see Kohn 1969). Most responded with a mixture of hope and apprehension. Many parents worried that their children were increasingly exposed to influences and potential dangers outside the family, while their own ability to protect and guide them waned.

En route to adulthood

The term 'adolescence' immediately conjures up the notion of young people on the verge of adulthood, with all the drama and adjustment which that transition entails. In contrast, the phrases 'middle childhood' or 'primary school years' imply little other than a firm location in childhood, yet parents' accounts challenged this notion.

This 'stage' was not so much seen as a prelude to the teen years, but as marking the beginnings of adolescence, at least from about the age of ten onwards. At eight children were still seen as children, but by twelve they were adolescent and on the verge of the adult world. A number of parents expressed this very clearly:

> I would say that, especially for girls…you know, quite a few of them seem to change and start to begin to develop about eleven and I see a marked change from when, you know, at eight they're still children. Nine, ten they've gradually, by eleven they're beginning to be quite different, they're beginning to be like an adult more than a child I would say. I would say it's possibly quite different with the boys. I think the boys are certainly behind.
>
> They're a very independent group. Get to the stage where they say, 'Get in the background Mum'. They don't want you interfering too much. But very insecure. Very cheeky. Not so much the eight-year-olds – more the twelve-year-olds, because that's when you see them become more cheeky, more assertive, but you still see that they're very vulnerable – so long as you're there in the background. But they try to become their own person. They realise that they need their space and they start to speak to you as if you're their equal… You see them growing up. And you see them changing so much.

This period of childhood was seen as a time when children bridged the gap between child and adult worlds. They changed in themselves and relationships with adults altered in ways which might more usually be associated with teenagers. The same individual showed both child and adult characteristics, so children might be clingy and 'childlike' one day and fiercely independent the next:

I think it's the start of the wanting to be independent and alternatively clinging to you at the same time. I think they are wanting to actually go out and do their own thing and be this big person. They think they can manage it. But they also get very scared and at the same time they want you to help – so there's a lot of struggling that goes on at that time, and I think it does happen earlier than we think.

We tend to associate that with teenagers, and – I don't think – I think its roots are earlier. I think it definitely starts earlier.

With the onset of puberty, children, particularly girls, were described as becoming more emotional and sensitive in response to changes in hormones and their body shape. Opinions varied as to when these changes might start. Some parents explained personality changes from as young as eight in terms of puberty, but others saw eleven as an almost universal time of rapid change in girls. There was virtually unanimous agreement that boys' physical, social and sexual development was slower than girls. On the other hand both boys and girls were said to be equally concerned about their body image and required as much support.

Though they identified a range of social and emotional pressures children faced during these middle years, parents identified three main aspects as most salient:

- peer pressures
- dangers from unknown adults
- the need to do well academically and ultimately find employment.

Thus parents' perception of this stage as inherently difficult for children was to some extent based on worries about what the future might hold as much as on immediate concerns.

Preparation for adult life

A key perception was that preparation for adult life was already vital at this age. Many expressed a sense of regret that children had to be prepared so thoroughly at this early stage for the dangers and challenges of the adult world. This was seen as resulting in a loss of innocence which prevented children from experiencing the kind of carefree lives which most of the parents recalled from their own childhoods. Almost every aspect of the children's lives was evaluated for its 'insurance' potential for the future. There was pressure to succeed at school in order to lay the foundations for securing employment. Activities such as swimming or karate were valued not only for their enjoyment and sense of achievement, but because children were developing relationships with like-minded young people whose influence would pose less of a threat in the future. Many more children were viewed as 'easily led' than as leaders, and peers were mostly viewed as a potential hazard. There was little sense of parents simply enjoying the current activities and achievements of their children: the present was very much coloured by anticipation and often foreboding about the future.

In some respects this stage was seen as a 'last chance' to influence children before they became teenagers when parents could expect to have an even less prominent role in their lives. The image of children moving away from the home sphere was a strong one, with the move to secondary school being a major step on this road. There was a sense in which children were seen as inhabiting an increasingly separate world from adults. This entailed not only more physical apartness, but also increasing divergence of experience and knowledge. An example was that parents felt particularly excluded from the drug culture which they knew their children would encounter, or were indeed already in touch with.

If mid-childhood was seen as a difficult stage, the impending teen years were viewed as even more hazardous. Parents were keenly aware that they had to prepare children not only for adult life but to negotiate adolescence. Certain parents dreaded their children moving into this age group: some feared for their children facing the dangers of the outside world, others were sad at losing the close involvement they had had in their children's lives. The parents adhered to the widely held view of the family and home as a 'haven in a heartless world' (Lasch 1977) and, while recognising that sooner or later children would have to move into the outside world, they viewed this as a threatening domain, particularly during adolescence. These anxieties applied to parents from all three geographical areas.

I don't want mine to get older

— Aye that worries me a lot. I don't want him to be a fighter or be in trouble, I want him to go through school without anybody seeing him if you know what I mean. Just like just get him past that age to where like he's an adult. I think it's quite worrying.

Reciprocity and communication

If there were worries and perceived drawbacks to children getting older, there were also real advantages. Children in mid-childhood were seen as more able to understand and respond to the needs of others which promoted reciprocity in their relationships with adults. Perhaps inevitably, examples usually referred to situations involving some adversity. Instances were cited of children caring for parents who were ill. Virtually all of the parents who had separated referred to how their children were sensitive to the feelings of the key adults concerned and modified their behaviour and conversation to protect or care for their parents. One father who no longer lived with his son described how the boy tried to hide the fact that he now called his mother's partner 'dad'. A mother who saw her twelve-year-old son at weekends explained that he did not phone her too often in between because he knew his father needed the security of knowing he was the main parent in his life. Another separated father who continued to care for his three children also acknowledged their awareness of his needs:

> At times they know I need a wee bit of warmth and affection. And it's not that they come up and sit on your knee because they're wanting a cuddle from daddy, they know that dad needs a cuddle from them.

From around age eight children were seen as much more able to discuss with parents, to understand the reasons for people's actions and have an appreciation of what was right and wrong, as cognitive psychology has also reported (Meadows 1990). Thus when there were family crises, such as parental separation, children asked for detailed explanations and wanted to be more involved in adult conversations. A mother who no longer lived with her child had found leaving the family easier because she was able to explain her reasons to her son, while a single father contrasted his eight-year-old's keen interest in why his mother had left with the younger daughter's apparent acceptance of simple explanations:

> He was beginning to look for more than one word, simple answers [...] When they get to that certain age they start to question. He worked out his own logic. He began to work out an awful lot for himself, and he had to have a proper answer. He more or less would ply his questions.

Girls were often described as very talkative at this age. Some were portrayed as talking non-stop. They would relate the events of the day to their parents in great detail. One group of mothers thought that this was an important means of checking out whether what they had done or said with friends had been appropriate. Children also used discussion with parents to work out their opinions and values on particular issues. Increased interest in and ability to understand other people's and wider social problems was seen as a characteristic of this age group.

However, the ability to discuss and debate in more detail was not always accompanied by a willingness to do so. As parents compared and contrasted descriptions of their children in the groups, several pointed out that this chatty 'gossip' image did not apply to all daughters, some of whom who were more private and remote. Neither were all boys seen as particularly chatty. Some parents were finding their sons less willing to confide in them and under more pressure to present a 'macho' image among peers. The tendency for more girls than boys to be concerned with personal conversation and relationships is well documented in the literature (Gordon and Grant, 1997; Hartup 1992).

Children as individuals

As parents discussed their children, the differences were as striking as the commonalities. Many were conscious of social factors and some groups debated the impact of class, income, family composition, individual experience and so on. Several parents also adhered to the view that children's individual personalities were more or less fixed from birth. Parents who had brought up several children were the strongest proponents of this argument about innate sibling differences (see Dunn and Plomin 1990). The case in favour of this viewpoint was put most convincingly by two grandparents who were caring for their grandson:

> Well we had four boys and four girls, eleven grandchildren and two great grandchildren...it's amazing all the different natures. People who've only got one or two, they don't see that. But when you've got eight of a family, it's amazing how they've all got different natures, and you've got to contend with that.

The idea that children's personalities were to some extent predetermined is prominent in the early years of parenthood (Hill 1987) but also featured strongly in the discussions of middle childhood, partly because people believed that individual personalities came to the fore then. One group of suburban parents who agreed that a child's personality could change dramatically around age eleven to twelve, debated whether this was due to inherent traits reaching fruition, the move to secondary school or the influence of friends. Not surprisingly, there were no clear answers. Probably each of these factors plays a part.

Parents thus saw mid-childhood as a time when children's needs and emotions were complex and sometimes contradictory. Children were striving for independence yet still needing 'loads of reassurance', becoming more able to discuss and communicate with parents, but keen to create some space for themselves. It was a stressful time, though also a time of activity, experimenting, excitement and opportunity.

Children on middle childhood

So how did these parental images of middle childhood match what children had told us about their lives? The exuberance of the children who took part in our parallel study was convincing evidence that their lives were indeed exciting, if also sometimes fraught. We did not directly ask the children in the Well-being study about life in middle childhood as such, but were interested in their understanding and experience of emotions and how adults should best promote children's well-being. Of course they responded to these questions as individuals and groups currently in the mid-childhood phase of life. When debating the topics, their reflections on their own experience provided glimpses of what life was like for them which, though not directly comparable, can be viewed alongside the parents' images. More direct questions about life at home were put to the smaller number of children who took part in the parenting study.

Developing through middle childhood

Though some common themes and concerns applied generally, an eight-year-old's life is clearly quite different from that of a young person approaching their teens. Here we summarise some of the differences before going on to identify common themes.

Developmental psychology points to the growing capacity of children as they get older to expand, reflect, decentre and generalise (Bee 1995). These features were evident from the interviews and there was also signs of a shift from the immediate and concrete, and from personal gain to altruistic concern for others. In other words, the children we interviewed were not unusual.

The developmental shift was gradual, and, of course, within it there were children who showed features of a more advanced stage of awareness, and others who were functioning at a younger level. Nevertheless, the changes were quite marked at the 'snapshot stages' we sampled.

The primary 1 children (aged about five years) in the Well-being study were mostly concerned with their own immediate and concrete needs and advantage, when telling us what made them feel happy or sad. For them happiness was mostly about getting sweets, toys and trips to MacDonalds, while unhappiness lay largely in having those things denied. Primary 3 children (aged about seven) were already showing signs of the shift to relationships and achievement, and were aware of a widening social network. Happiness was now concerned with family holidays, activities of various kinds and having friends to play. Negative emotions were becoming more complex and relationship-based. Punishment and reprimands by parents were now sometimes resented and a cause of anger. Deaths of grandparents and pets were also upsetting. This also seemed to be a peak period for fears which are seen as irrational by adults but which appeared vividly real to some children, for example nightmares, and visions of ghosts.

The primary 5s (around nine years old) confirmed a growing consciousness of the importance of relationships. Having friends was a vital constituent of happiness, losing them the most common source of misery. Events involving other relatives besides parents were assuming more central positions, for example visiting extended family, the birth of a sibling. Adults were losing their aura of omnipotence and omniscience, and were discovered to have feet of clay, so that unfair treatment by parents and teachers was now a major source of anger. Activities and achievements were a vital part of life: clubs, sports, competitions. Fears were now becoming more reality-based: bullies – both in and out of school; parental arguments; being left alone in the house.

Primary 7s (eleven- to twelve-year-olds) in many ways simply carried on at a more sophisticated level the concerns of the primary 5s. Friends were still central, and now in many circumstances the major confidants. Individual and family issues were still important, but group identity and achievements were increasingly important. This was illustrated by excitement and concerns about wearing the right clothes, team successes in football, taking part in school concerts and competitions, graduation to secondary school. Children were now much more critical of adults, and discriminated between them: some teachers could be trusted to deal with a situation, others were regarded as ineffectual. Children of this age were more choosy about who they turn to for help, and recognised that this varies with the problem concerned. They were much more aware of adult concerns, and saw their parents' limitations more clearly. They acknowledged that mums and dads, too, have problems they can't solve and may need support from their children.

For some at least, a sense of injustice extended to the wider world, and some of the children were angry and distressed by wars, world hunger, racism, poverty, homelessness and cruelty to animals. Given the chance they would try to help with these issues too. A few children were starting to worry about the challenges facing them in the future: the demands of secondary school, the hazards of drugs and unprotected sex. Despite this, by and large it was a good time of life, with ever-expanding horizons, impatience for independence, and a sense of mastery and excitement.

Boys and girls

When they themselves discussed gender, children often made definite statements about the differences between boys and girls, though there was often disagreement about how true the generalisations were. Amongst the suggested contrasts were:

- boys show their emotions less than girls
- girls feel more sadness, whereas boys are more indifferent to loss
- boys are rougher
- boys are less inclined to apologise
- boys boast more
- girls fall out more than boys
- girls are more likely to blame themselves and admit they are in the wrong
- girls are more likely to confide (or, in boys' terms, tell tales).

Some individuals demonstrated stereotyped attitudes:

> Crying is for lassies.

> You're not a girl, you don't understand — We're girls, we understand.

In all-male groups, there was some evidence of boys living up to a tough, unfeeling image, but boys in mixed groups came over quite differently. They admitted to both positive and negative feelings, talked about upsetting experiences with feeling, and showed empathy and concern for others. Most boys in individual interviews also showed these qualities. Though caution is needed with such small numbers, it may be that in a group situation, girls may have a strong influence on boys, facilitating emotional disclosure and eliciting caring responses. The presence of other boys may equally have a powerful influence in inhibiting them. Our experience may thus confirm what some of the older girls claimed:

> See if there's a big crowd of boys in our class...and an old woman walks up, they'd like, kinda fling stones at her, and everything, and act horrible to her. But see if they were by themselves, they wouldn't act like that. They'd just walk right by her — Boys are scared to show their emotions... I mean, say some boy like J went up to an old lady and helped her along, and told the boys 'Stop carrying on. You're being a bunch of idiots'. They would all turn round and go like that: 'Whit?!' and they would start fighting him ... — They think everything's a joke. There's this boy in our class called C and when he's with a group of boys, right, they all muck about and are pains in the backside and everything, but, em, I walk, sometimes I walk the same way as C, and we just talk about things, and treat each other as equals. He's like a different person ... When they're in a big group, they just fight and everything.

Ethnic minority children

We were particularly concerned to see whether there were any significant differences in the approach to feelings among children from ethnic minority groups, and to that end were careful to include children of Chinese and Asian origin in both groups and individual interviews. By contrast with parts of England, Scotland has very few children of Afro-Caribbean heritage.

We found few readily apparent differences among children in the groups. Individual interviews elicited a few. Asian children, as might be expected, had very close links with their extended families, and thus there was more involvement of grandparents, aunts and uncles at times of family crisis. Children would sometimes speak of a favourite aunt or uncle (sometimes not much older than them) as a particular confidant. They also seemed to have close relationships with parents, particularly mothers. Since the children we spoke to also seemed well integrated into their peer groups, with friends of varied ethnic backgrounds, it appears that some British-Asian children may be particularly well supported in times of stress.

Friendship

Perhaps the key feature to emerge from the children's discussions was that friendship and being part of the peer group were central to living a full life and feeling good. Older children more than younger children cited friendships as a main source of both positive and negative feelings. Close personal friendships were a particularly important source of happiness and support, especially for girls. Many children spoke of discussing worries with their friends or gave examples of being helped to cope with sadness and loss. Conversely, friends could also be a source of considerable distress. This theme is developed in Chapter 8.

In the majority of groups and in most individual interviews, friends and acquaintances were portrayed as those with the most power to hurt. However, this appeared to vary with age as well as gender. For younger children peer relationships seemed more diffuse and upsets with 'best friends' more transitory, while for older children, particularly girls, difficulties with friendships and peers often evoked very intense and troubled emotions (see Berndt 1986; Ganetz 1995). In addition to retaining special, close friends, it was important to be part of the wider group. 'No one playing with you' and 'having no friends' were conditions to be avoided at all costs. Befriending a friendless child was both viewed as altruistic and as something many would seek to do.

Thus relationships with peers were central to children's well-being in ways which parents perhaps only partially understood. While many parents recognised the importance of friendships and being part of the peer group, they also tended to be suspicious of peer influence rather then to value it. They also appeared to underestimate how distressed children could be when friendships turned sour.

Boundaries with the adult world

Parents only partially understood the children's world outside the home and the rules and rituals which governed it. Aware of this and of adults' potential power, some children were wary of involving adults in peer disputes or concerns. Although most children saw most adults as helpful and benign, there was territory which was only for children. As one group agreed:

> Children can help each other, though. Adults can't do that because they don't know what they're feeling — ... They don't understand children cos they've grown out of it — ... Sometimes parents just try and lead your life and they'll say 'you can just go and play with that one over there.'

Even if parents were understanding, confidentiality among and loyalty towards friends sometimes required their exclusion:

> Sometimes it's easiest to talk to parents, but it depends what you're thinking about... Well, say you've seen something that shouldn't be done, right, but you don't want to get your friends into trouble, so you don't really want to talk to your parents about that [But] if you're getting bullied or that, you would want to talk to your parents about it.

While, in some respects children guarded their separateness, in other ways they felt excluded from the adult world. Even some quite young children described occasions when they were concerned because their parents had been upset and they had not known the reason. Unsurprisingly, with no other explanation to hand, a few blamed themselves for their parent's worries or conflicts. Marital discord worried several children and some thought their anxiety was greater because their parents did not explain their differences or discuss their problems in their presence. However opinions varied and some were not keen to be fully informed of adult worries. A few felt overburdened by parental sharing and others did not want the responsibility which too much knowledge might confer:

> I'd probably get a wee bit worried about it — like say I'd better not ask my parents for trainers and I need a pair...if they were having financial problems.

Though ambivalence about growing up was expressed in a number of ways, children were generally optimistic about the future and did not seem as troubled or vulnerable, as some parents felt they were. Virtually all primary 7 children were looking forward to going to secondary school, while being given more responsibility and freedom was cited by some as a source of great pleasure. In fact several children thought life was much easier for them than for adults, if only because they had their parents on hand to confide in:

> I don't think adult people go to another adult and talk to her about it, you know... Like if my wee brother did something angry to me...upsetting, then I tell my mum, and my mum will do something about it, but if, you know, my mum did something to my dad, then my dad cannot tell anyone, you know?

Most children seemed to accept the ups and downs of their own lives, while playing their part in shaping what happened to them and others.

Children as active participants in shaping their own lives

Children have sometimes been portrayed as passively following lifepaths and activities determined by adults, and so as mere products of socialisation by parents, schools, social class and so on (James and Prout 1990). Those in our studies described numerous ways in which they made choices or took action which affected their own and others well-being. There were many examples of children helping or being supported by their friends and some were honest enough to talk about how they made life difficult for other people. There were also many tales of perceived unfairness which children felt powerless to challenge, but as they became more articulate, there was the possibility of more dialogue with the people in charge. One primary 7 boy described how he was consulted about how an episode of bullying should be tackled:

> They [Parents] say, well, they ask me 'Do you want me to handle it?' [Bullying] I usually say I'll handle it first, and then if I can't get them to stop, I go and talk to them.

Naturally parents differed in the extent to which they were willing to engage in this kind of negotiation or allow their children to take the lead.

Several children illustrated their active participation in family life with accounts of the practical ways in which they helped out at home, often when parents were ill or needed care. One girl talked about massaging her mother's back and another took over the basic chores:

> I do the dishes and tidy the living room up when my mum's not well. And I try not to make a noise 'cause I always tell her to go to bed and get a rest. And I make good dishes. I make her dinner 'cause I've got a wee microwave and I use that.

Another nine-year-old described her part in the normal family routine:

> My dad usually comes in about 5.30 or 6.30 or 6 o'clock. And my mum, she makes the dinner for my dad. And my dad does the dishes and I dry them. And then it's time for my wee brother to get his pyjamas on. So I usually get him ready and my dad puts him to bed.

Though these examples are from girls, there were also boys who helped with hoovering and cooking. There was little evidence that these children resented having to help at home, though it is possible that they preferred to present themselves as willing rather than reluctant helpers. Other studies have reported that, for many children, responsibility for household chores and/or care of a relative are an accepted part of normal life (Aldridge and Becker 1995; Hill 1992; Newson and Newson 1976). For the children we met, this did not seem to detract from their general enjoyment of life.

Middle childhood from the inside

On the outside, most of the children we met were enjoying life, though their lives were not completely carefree. This was apparent in discussions with children who took part in both studies. Talking about their understanding of emotional well-being also offered glimpses of what life felt like for children of this age 'on the inside'.

Recognising emotions

Children from age six to twelve engaged enthusiastically in discussion about feelings, showing ability to identify a wide range of emotions and to reflect on what circumstances might provoke them and how they might be experienced. Not surprisingly, older children's ideas were more detailed and sophisticated, so that when asked what emotions might be inferred from six cardboard faces they were shown, a group of primary 7 boys produced the following list:

- happy, smiley, cheerful, glad, proud, jolly
- cross, angry, grumpy, moody, frustrated, upset, sad, annoyed, unhappy
- surprised, shocked, frightened, amazed, overjoyed
- crying, unhappy, sad, lonely, depressed, overworked, tired, downhearted, down in the dumps

- angry, moody, cross, unsure, lost, frightful, not understanding what to do
- frightened, scared, shocked, terrified, worried, alarmed, nervous, now knowing what to do, rooted to the spot.

The variety of responses given in relation to the same face illustrates that there are some differences in interpretation of more ambiguous expressions. In particular, there are indications that externally directed feelings like anger may be confused with internalised emotions like sadness and uncertainty. If transferred to real life situations, this could lead to misunderstandings.

One group added other feelings which can't be seen from faces:

- heartbroken, hurt (by what someone said), trapped, jealous, lonely, bored, unwanted, having nobody who likes you.

While these are all negative, other groups of primary 7 children identified positive hidden feelings such as love, thoughtfulness, caring. The older ones, it seemed, were likely to identify more complex interactive emotions like jealousy and loneliness, but otherwise the range of emotions identified by most children were broadly comparable.

Children were not only able to recognise feelings from facial expressions but could point to other signs of how people feel, notably posture and gesture. For instance, holding your head down was recognised as an expression of sadness or shame, quietness as an indicator of nervousness.

The children also talked about typical sequences of feelings. Thus, irritation with a friend may quickly give way to remorse and a wish to make up. Grumpiness on waking up may wear off as the day progresses. Anxiety or embarrassment about a public performance can lead on to satisfaction or excitement once it is over.

Showing and hiding emotions

As some parents lamented, it is not always easy to know what a child is feeling nor to read accurately the signs from what they say and do. Children were aware from an early age that feelings can be hidden and that there can be benefits from pretending. Negative feelings could be masked for the sake of other adults or children:

They could be happy outside, but they could be sad inside

If their mummy wanted them to be happy, maybe they were just pretending to be happy. Because they didn't want their mum to know that they were sad.

> I'm quite popular with the wee ones…and sometimes I get angry when they keep coming up to me, but I just keep a smile on. [Why?] Because I don't want to frighten them, because I like them, and they're cute.

On the other hand, it was recognised that feelings can be indirectly expressed, sometimes resulting in unacceptable and and/or counterproductive behaviour:

> If someone was miserable, scared, cross with themselves…they wouldn't act like they normally would… They would maybe be more cheeky — Or angry.

> If I'm upset, sometimes my Mum says I'm rude…and she doesn't listen to me…and she just gets angry, so sometimes I get angry as well.

Envy or jealousy figured either explicitly or implicitly in several group discussions, reflecting the great significance of social comparison amongst peers. Children admitted to resentments at others who spoke about possessions or experiences they lacked themselves, for example having a new pet. It was recognised that other children could feel 'sad cos they don't have one', but that:

> They shouldn't say 'I haven't got that — that's not fair'. They should say 'That's good. What's his name?'

This showed a good awareness of the tensions between honest self-expression and altruistic promotion of other's well-being. In general the children had a sophisticated appreciation of their own feelings but they were also increasingly aware of others' emotional needs and of how interaction between the two affected their well-being and peace of mind. The balance they settled for between their own and others' needs no doubt varied, reflecting different parental and societal expectations.

Summary

For the parents we saw, middle childhood was a period of concern, mainly about external threats to their children's well-being. They also described difficulties in managing their children's increased questioning and desire for more freedom. In general the children we met seemed to be enjoying life and conveyed a quite sophisticated understanding of their emotional and social world. They did not share their parents' worries about the future or even to the same degree about current hazards outside the home. The desire to give socially acceptable responses may have contributed to the broadly positive image the children conveyed, yet some of their comments did indicate a willingness to talk about undesirable thoughts or behaviour. In addition, the requirement for parental consent may have excluded the most troubled or isolated children from our sample. Nevertheless, though essentially happy, those we met were not trouble-free. Whereas parents were preoccupied with dangers in the outside world, children's worries centred much more on personal relationships with family and friends. There was no doubt that parents remained key people in the children's lives and we now move on to consider how they fared, judged from their own and the children's perspective.

CHAPTER 3

The Grown-up Pains of Parenthood

Parents on parenting in middle childhood

Introduction

Asking parents to talk about parenting might be likened to asking a lorry driver about driving: it is a skilled activity which is central to their lives, yet much of what it involves seems 'natural' and is not routinely analysed. Parents are unaccustomed to turning the spotlight on themselves and when we asked about the task of parenting, most replied in terms of their children's needs. This is not surprising; as Jackson, Fischer and Ward (1996) pointed out, the word 'parenting' is of very recent origin, first appearing in the Oxford English Dictionary in 1970, though people have always argued about the best way to bring up children.

In recent years, a wide array of programmes and projects have been established to prepare, educate and support both 'ordinary' parents and parents who have particular problems (Gibbons 1995; Pugh, De'Ath and Smith 1994). In addition more targeted services have been developed to assist parents who are under pressure and to provide the elements of good parental care when local authorities take on some responsibility for children's care (Parker *et al.* 1991; Ward 1995). The research and debate which informed these developments concluded that 'parenting' is an inclusive term which encompasses everything that parents do to promote their children's development and well-being throughout childhood and into adult life. For some purposes it may be helpful to distinguish parenthood as embodying general responsibilities which reside legally with one or both parents and parenting which encompasses the daily tasks of caring for children, some of which may be shared or taken on by 'non-parents' (Hill 1991).

The key characteristics of parenting have been defined as being (Jackson *et al.* 1995):

- concerned with responsibilities not rights

- not specific to gender

- not confined to adults with a biological relationship with the child

- open-ended. It changes its nature as children mature but may well continue into adulthood

- including the active promotion of children's welfare, both in the present and with a view to their longer term well-being

- acting as an advocate for the child as necessary

- a two way process, in that the way parents behave is influenced by the characteristics of the child as well as the other way round.

These characteristics are consistent with the concept of parenting which is given expression in children's legislation which now governs each part of the United Kingdom. These define parental responsibilities and recognise the rights of children as active participants whose welfare is to be the primary consideration. Although mostly unaware of legal developments, parents' discussions about what they did in practice reflected many of these officially sanctioned characteristics, while at the same time highlighting some of the tensions which accompany changing expectations.

In this chapter we outline what parents of eight- to twelve-year-olds said the job entailed – a kind of job description. We also report the ways in which parents described their parental functions in a range of situations and roles, including some who are not living with their children. Unfortunately not enough step-parents took part in the study to allow their important perspective to be represented (for further information see Ochiltree 1990; Dimmock 1997/8).

Parental tasks

Unsurprisingly, the job of parenting children aged eight to twelve had much in common with being a parent to older or younger children, yet also changed throughout the years of middle childhood. The essential parental task was to meet the needs of their children. These were seen by parents in similar ways as in studies based on professional and academic perspectives (Pringle 1980; Pugh *et al.* 1995; Stolz 1967), namely love, security, praise and positive experiences. Children's needs were still primarily seen as being met within the home or family domain but friends and activities outwith the home also had a role.

Table 3.1 shows the parental tasks which were identified and which might be seen as corresponding with five aspects of children's needs.

Table 3.1 Parental Tasks

Need	Tasks/responsibilities
Emotional	listen, give reassurance, support, boost confidence, encourage, provide stability and security, give love and attention.
Moral/social	teach right from wrong, teach respect for self, other people and material belongings, help learn to get on with other people, help learn about people from different backgrounds, discipline, set defined limits, 'referee' sibling disputes.
Physical	cook, monitor diet, keep clean, nurse when ill, monitor health and get medical advice when necessary, keep children safe.
Educational	keep in contact with school, help extend general knowledge, supervise homework.
Recreational	encourage in activities, transport or accompany child to activities, engage in joint activities.

In addition to meeting these specific tasks, parents, usually mothers, performed an overseeing role, ensuring that different kinds of needs were met and that no one aspect of their children's lives was neglected. Most parents saw children's needs as interrelated and aimed to care for the 'whole' child so that many tasks were carried out across the three domains of home, school and the outside world. Thus emotional support might take the form of listening to children's worries, arranging for them to join a club or advocating with school staff on their behalf.

The overarching tasks were care for children and keeping them safe at present, while preparing them for the future and enabling them to become independent. The basic mechanisms for doing this were described as provision of support and reassurance combined with setting boundaries and discipline.

of support and reassurance combined with setting boundaries and discipline. Specific tasks might involve direct care, back-up support or helping bridge the gap with the outside world. To perform these tasks, parents said that tact, self-control and negotiation skills were important requirements. Parenting a child aged eight to twelve was thought to be more difficult than caring for a younger child, because both parental influence and the hoped-for outcomes were often more indirect and at a distance:

> I think children of all ages need, you know sort of security, stability, home comforts, somebody there to put the meals on the table, clean up after them, that sort of thing. But as they get older there's things like encouraging them in their development and to explore the world.

> They need loads of support but not a lot of interference. Just stand back, support them. I think it's really important that they go out and get – they need an awful lot of freedom and they also have to be safe, so you've got to try and manufacture a situation where they can go out and be with friends but also going and coming in safely.

Though no clear patterns emerged to indicate that parents of different gender, class or family structures had fundamentally different ideas about parental tasks, some differences in emphasis were identified. For example, aspects of physical care were discussed in more detail by parents from the peripheral scheme and rural area than by the suburban parents and by women more often than men. Discipline and control issues were important for all parents but featured less prominently in discussions with suburban parents. However it did not seem that the middle-class parents were less controlling than the others, rather they took for granted being in charge.

Being a mother and being a father

There is a popular perception that fathers are more involved in parenting nowadays than they were in the past, yet closer scrutiny has usually revealed that women still have responsibility for most of the housework and child care (Lewis and O'Brien 1987; Moss 1995). This study indicated that many stereotypical beliefs continue to have currency and that being a mother is quite different from being a father.

Despite the fact that several women paid tribute to their husband's patience and sensitivity and several fathers described talking with children about their worries, there was a general belief that women were better at providing emotional support than men. Another belief was that fathers were naturally more authoritarian whereas women were able to negotiate, a skill which was considered very important at this stage. Again several parents said this did not apply to themselves, but they thought of themselves as unusual in this respect and so indicated this belief was valid within their social circle.

Men were also thought to be practically less competent with children, for example they would leave the stair gate open when children were young, and less able to perform the 'management' aspects of parenting. A mother said:

> I don't know if it's physiological, but you can juggle a few things in your head at the time, my husband can think of only one thing, and that's it.

Mothers' ability to 'juggle a few things in your head' or keep an overview was mentioned quite often, so that, even when men were actively involved in specific activities, women retained overall responsibility:

> I think we can take an equal share in certain household tasks but there are still – if he's in he'll do the dinner but by silent agreement I am the one who will always check that homework's done, I'm the one who will always check that dental appointments are being kept, even if it's not me that takes the child, I'm the one that has to keep the log in my head.

Similarly some single mothers meeting in a group said that, though men sometimes helpfully took on the responsibility of discussing sex education with their sons, it was usually the mothers who prompted them to do so.

Responsibility was one of the components of fathering identified by Lamb, the other key elements being interaction and availability (Lamb 1987). Responsibility is about ensuring the child is taken care of and arranging for resources to be available; interaction refers to direct contact with the child through caregiving and shared activities; and availability means being in each other's company.

Interaction and availability of fathers were largely, though not entirely, influenced by whether or not the father was working. Some fathers who worked long hours had very little contact with their children. A mother of three children remarked:

> I think perhaps the men would like to be more involved. I know my husband would, but…he works all the hours there are, really, and I feel he can't make commitments to the children that he would like to do – about the only time he gets that chance is on holiday… I haven't been working, so it's still my job.

However some fathers themselves described quite strenuous efforts to make time for their children, engaging in activities with them at weekends or just trying to be patient and responsive despite being tired in the evenings.

Both mothers and fathers commented that tasks were more evenly divided when both or neither parent worked. A few fathers talked about being much more involved with their children since they had become unemployed and acknowledged with regret that they had missed a lot of their children's early years, partly because they had been working long hours and partly because they had not realised how enjoyable their children's company could be.

Traditional differences between the sexes were reflected in the ways many mothers and fathers spent time with their children. Typically mothers and daughters went shopping whereas fathers took boys to the football. Although there were variations in how parents complemented each other, overall fathers had a more active role outside the home while mothers' were more influential at home. Even where fathers said the responsibilities were equally shared, they talked more about outside activities than domestic chores. As one father put it:

> When anything happens in the house the kids go straight to my wife, anything outside the house that's my role, that's where I come in. It's 'dad, what's this'... So for my bairns anything to do with the outdoors anything to do with outside the house, that's 'we need dad'. I'm no the most affectionate person, my bairns, I'm just like, I try to be as strong, as reliable as I can be for the bairns.

This father's comments also highlight that mothers and fathers might show love or care for the children in different ways, a point also made by some children.

Thus the families in our study did not present a significant challenge to the widely held view that women remain key players in relation to children's well-being (Mayall 1994b). On the whole, women did not indicate that they resented having this responsibility. In fact a number of mothers acknowledged that they liked to be in control. For example:

> The reason that I would probably do it is because I take it upon myself. Although you do think that they have their bit that they can contribute, you still, in your heart, it's really, that's my domain, whether you like it or not. I know that I always like to, I hate to have a feeling, in a way selfish, of not being in control, you know, from that aspect, I don't really care too much if the house is a mess but I like to have the bit of control.

Though too few to be necessarily typical, our interviews themselves lent a degree of support to the idea that women might unwittingly restrict men's parenting role. Whereas, in mixed groups or in the company of their partner, men tended to defer to the woman's superior knowledge, they portrayed themselves as more active and thoughtful parents when interviewed alone or along with other men. Evidently long-held views and patterns of behaviour are difficult to challenge and slow to change.

Lone parenting

When there was only one parent, the role of mother or father took on a different perspective. The assumption that women are more natural and capable parents than men led to some single fathers feeling reasonably well-supported because there were regular offers of help from neighbours and friends who thought it a tall order to be a lone father.

On the down side, one lone father felt people expected him to be exclusively preoccupied with his children and fathering duties, forgetting he was also a person in his own right. Similarly a group of single mothers also talked about always putting their children first, so that their own needs became eclipsed:

> Since you've become a parent, you're not 'you' in your own right any more — You don't have priorities for yourself, they're the priority 'cause you've got to always put them first — And you keep worrying are you doing the right thing / How often do we all save up for something and you've got the money and you think great and you go out and then the wean comes back and needs a pair of shoes and you think 'I don't need it I can do without it'.

Thus rather than being irresponsible, as lone parents are sometimes portrayed in the media, the people we met were highly committed to promoting their children's welfare. Despite this commitment, one single father felt he could not compensate for his wife's absence:

> He's missing out, he's missing out on his mum's influence. There's no two ways about it. As I say, I can only be as good a dad as possible. I can't be a mum.

Some lone mothers also thought their children, particularly their sons, missed out if no father was around, especially at this age when they were keen to take part in traditional male activities, such as going to football matches. Others relied on uncles or grandfathers to provide a role model, male companionship and an occasional 'firm hand'.

On the whole, people who had a partner conveyed more negative images of lone parenthood than did single parents themselves. The couples tended to think only in terms of young single mothers and dwelt on the presumed stress and lack of support. In contrast lone parents themselves, while recognising the difficulties, quite often described themselves as resilient, referred to supportive links with other adults and liked having control over how they managed their home. A few married mothers who had also experienced single parenthood confirmed that, financial considerations apart, there could be some advantages to being on your own.

Parenting when apart

The notion of continuing parental responsibility is now enshrined in legislation governing each part of the United Kingdom, so that parents who are not living with their children will increasingly have the opportunities, and sometimes be required, to find ways of continuing to be a parent while living elsewhere. This is a new challenge for parents. As with step-parenting, there are few clear rules and no 'script' as yet about what parenting at a distance should entail (Burgoyne and Clark 1984).

From the comments of lone and non-resident parents, it was clear that bitter disagreements often made joint parenting difficult after parents split up. Though eight- to twelve-year-old's increasing capacity to express their views potentially increased the likelihood that their parents would take their wishes into account, it could also put them under pressure to find the words to please both parents. There were several accusations that one parent 'used' children in battles with the other and numerous examples of children adapting what they said and did to protect their parents and keep the peace. In some instances it seemed that children anticipated parental competition which sensitive parents picked up and responded to. A single father illustrated this:

> I says, 'Look, your mum loves you, and I love you, and I want you to love Mum, Mum wants you to love me. You've not to say, I love Daddy better, when you're talking to Daddy, or I love Mummy better, when you're talking to Mummy. You can love everybody... I think she was feeling, I'd better not speak about Mum too much when I'm with Dad.

Despite the difficulties, a range of joint arrangements were described. The most common pattern of contact was for mothers to continue to care for children while fathers visited the children in the family home or took them on outings. However one mother insisted that her estranged husband look after her children every evening to allow her to work and a non-resident father said he tried to oversee what was happening in his children's lives by checking with their head teacher that dental and medical appointments had been kept.

It was widely accepted that parents who were no longer living with their children lost authority to be a full parent. This view was expressed by non-resident parents and those continuing to care for the children, irrespective of whether the carer was male or female. A group of single mothers from a city scheme talked about how they regulated the kind of role their children's father could have with them. For example they might report children's misbehaviour to the father but would decide how he was allowed to respond (for example, by smacking them, giving them a row or stopping pocket money). Their view was that parents had to earn the right to have authority with children through being there and caring for them.

For some parents, limited involvement in their children's lives made it difficult for them to think of themselves as parents at all. A non-resident father described such a position:

> I don't think I really am a parent. I'm not a parent in the sense because I have not got K here constantly. I'm just a wee small part of his life. I see my son and he is my son and I'm his father – but as a parent and bringing him up, dressing him, getting him to school, feeding him, this, that and the next thing, I mean that is just not part of my life. I've just got a very small part of that boy's life.

The one non-custodial mother we saw was more content with her relationship with her son than the men. She enjoyed talking with her twelve-year-old son and found advantages in having a more equal rather than parenting relationship with him. However she also commented on her lack of parental authority, evidenced by having to negotiate extensively with her ex-husband to be allowed to take her son on holiday. She also found that other parents did not accept her authority and would check arrangements with his father even after she had agreed, for example, that their son would stay overnight with friends.

Non-resident parents were coping with the loss of their children, while at the same time trying to find ways of continuing to play a part in their lives by negotiation with the other parent. Sharing responsibility, a legal requirement of parents, was not easy. It seems to be difficult for people to accommodate new notions about what being a parent might entail, even when stereotypical notions do not accord with their own experience.

Influences on parenting

Household composition was only one factor which shaped how individuals carried out the job of being a parent. References to a host of other influences were made throughout the interviews, both spontaneously and in response to questions such as: whether boys and girls required different things from parents; what factors made the job of parenting easier or more difficult and what influenced parents' views of what the ideal father or mother should be like. Common influences identified related to:

1. the children

2. parents' expectations and personalities

3. external factors, notably the area families live in, income and the television.

Children's personality, birth order and gender

It has been recognised for some time that children are not passive recipients of parenting but shape how their parents respond (Bell 1970; Mayall 1994b). A common theme in parents' conversations was that parenting style had to be adjusted to suit each individual child. Parents had different views about the extent to which children's personalities were inherited or created. There was a fairly common view that some characteristics were innate while other people emphasised the importance of children's position in the family and experience. Explanatory beliefs based on birth order and the gender constellation within the family were common (see Hill 1987). Youngest children were commonly described as immature while oldest children were seen as either self-reliant or jealous, both being the result of having to relinquish parental attention when younger children were born. Single children were described as confident with adults and more prosocial than other children, though their single status was thought to elicit over-protective behaviour on the part of parents (see Laybourn 1994). Thus children's personality, their experience in the family and how they were parented were seen as interlinked.

While there was some recognition that children often changed as they progressed through childhood, there was a sense that each had persistent personality traits. The following dimensions were cited as important:

- active / passive
- cautious / keen to extend experience and take risks
- gregarious / solitary
- open, willing to talk / quiet and withdrawn
- challenging / compliant
- truthful / untruthful
- self-centred / other oriented
- confident / diffident.

Inevitably, parents evaluated their children's behaviour in relation to their own expectations, so that parents who expected and liked compliant, quiet children could be upset by a child who actively challenged, whereas others might welcome or admire such assertiveness. Children's behaviour was a major source of stress for some parents. There were accounts of constant insolent or aggressive behaviour and several parents described family life as a series of battles between siblings. Naturally, for others family life was much less fraught.

Views differed on whether boys and girls demanded different responses from parents. In some group discussions respondents frequently attributed significant gender differences and checked out with each other whether their experience confirmed them, whereas other parents emphasised each child's individuality. Some parents also indicated that their children were highly influenced by social pressures which introduced a new dimension to inter- actions with their parents. To illustrate how entrenched some stereotypes and expectations were, one mother described how her children challenged her attempts to treat her son and daughter equitably:

> Even though you try not to treat them differently, they are bringing in the differences from outside, maybe in terms of their age or their gender [agreement from other group members] and that way it's hard not to. I suspect I'm allowing my son to be a child for longer than I would my daughter, his older sister. It would be terrible to think that it's because he's a boy but I suspect it might be... He does do things like coming down with sad eyes. The dirty clothes, you know, saying 'Oh, gee, I'm so sorry', and you fall for it! I think it's a boy/mother thing, as it is a girl/father thing. I try very very hard, conscious of it as I am, not to take on the roles, but even though I try to treat them the same, they are coming in with their gender from outside and how they would behave.

Parents also talked about adjusting their way of relating to their children in response to their growing maturity. A frequently mentioned aspect was that fathers drew back from physical contact with their daughters as they became sexually mature, while with both boys and girls, rules and boundaries were increasingly negotiated rather than imposed. This is discussed more fully in Chapter 4.

Parents' expectations and personalities

Virtually everyone thought their own parents had influenced their ideas about parenting, either by providing a good example or one to react against. Sometimes other relatives or friends' parents had become alternative role models, if their own parents' style had been disliked. Interestingly, several men but only a few women said they had ideas about the kind of parent they would like to be before or shortly after the birth of their first child. For some women, trying to replicate their own mother's (perceived) standards of caring while also working full-time was a source of stress:

> We try to bring the same amount of mothering or caring in as your mother maybe did and that's where I think a lot of mothers get stressed because they try to do the two things equally as well and can't and therefore walk about with a guilt complex that you're not there all the time or whatever.

Dimensions of their own parenting which had been copied or changed included: expressing emotions more openly; providing encouragement rather than criticism; spending more time with children; openly sharing information rather than having lots of secrets; keeping children safe from abuse; earning children's respect and cooperation rather than demanding obedience. Underlying many accounts was a preference for more equal relationships with children and for greater emotional closeness than parents themselves had experienced. These emerged as the key aspirations of modern parents.

A few men and women talked about useful discussion programmes on television, or newspaper and magazine articles, but most people said their views had been shaped by their own or their partner's experience, rather than advice from others. Knowing how to be a good parent was seen by many people as common sense based on everyday life experience (see Backett 1982). One exception was a mother who had been sexually abused by her father and who had undergone extensive counselling before becoming a parent to try to ensure that she would not transfer any of her own pain to her children. Few other parents thought they needed special training for the job, though it was generally recognised that some adults were better equipped to be good parents than others. Patience, the ability to negotiate and enjoying being with children were regarded as important qualities.

External factors
THE PHYSICAL AND SOCIAL ENVIRONMENT

At a stage when many children were spending more time outwith the family sphere, the kind of area families lived in affected the crucial process of allowing children more freedom. Understandably, this was often more evident to us as we made visits to different areas than to families who often simply described their roles within the context of the particular neighbourhood they lived in. Those who had moved home were more conscious of the impact of variations in the physical and social environment. We found that parents made judgements about how safe their area was and this affected their level of stress and the degree to which they restricted their children's freedom. Busy roads and rivers were seen as hazards but so were isolated areas such as parks. Parents talked more frequently about social rather than physical dangers.

Parents who lived in the city schemes felt most unsafe while those living in the rural area felt most secure. Several parents said they had moved away from cities or towns to provide a better environment for their children's upbringing. Worries about safety affected all parents, but living in an area where you did not trust your neighbours created a particularly pervasive sense of threat. One woman compared her previous experience of living in a safe environment with her present situation:

When we lived in D, everybody's parents were the same. We could let them out in D and they could play all day and we would know if they weren't in one person's house they were in another person's house and they would know their children were *vice versa...*

They would know none of the children were going to be bullied by other children because it just didn't happen, you know. And if, by chance, it did happen if you went to say to the parents, you know, such and such happened today they would say, oh right, I'll get it sorted out and it was sorted out with no arguments. You didn't fight with any of the neighbours. But here it is just basically an upside down world. You know, it's like living somewhere out of the world.

The pressures of living in an 'upside down world' were described by many respondents from the city schemes. One couple echoed many other parents in expressing regret that there was no longer a sense of community. Several parents talked of suffering from depression which they attributed to the stress of living in an area with so many problems. A married couple living in a city scheme described how they saw their locality:

Mother : You can easily be swamped in an area like this because there's so much deprivation round about. You see it, I mean we've had old people dying in this close, simply because, well I say it was because there wasn't anyone in checking that particular morning, but across the way we had an old man lying for about two or three days simply because nobody checked on him. The community is no longer a community, we do not have, like the way it used to be where my mum stayed, used to leave your front door open. It's bolts and locks and chains and the kids sense that as well. The kids know that it's not a safe area.

Father : I mean it's not a community when the next door neighbour burgles your house. Somebody in the community is doing this and people know what's going on, you know, it can't be a proper community.

Mother : I mean the amount of alcohol in this area I think it's even with drugs, a lot of young people are selling drugs. Young mothers, 'cause maybe they owe money, they maybe need money lenders, a lot of social problems, there's a hell of a lot of social problems in this area, and if you were to just wallow in your own self-pity you would stay there with the rest of them.

In many ways the parenting task was more taxing for people who lived in unsafe areas. They were under considerable stress themselves and had to teach their children to cope with the hazards in their area. Reluctance to allow children out to play added to tensions at home. There were few local leisure facilities for children and few of the families had a car to reach clubs outwith the area. Recreational facilities are generally less available in disadvantaged areas (MacIntyre, MacIver and Soomans 1993).

Pleas for safe, well-supervised leisure facilities for the children were made by parents in both the city scheme and the rural area. Although the rural area was regarded as safe, some parents emphasised that children needed more stimulation than playing outside could offer. Others thought it was important that children learned to mix with a wider range of peers than the village children and so spent a lot of time and energy transporting children to clubs and activities in nearby towns. Not having a car would be a problem. The parents in the rural area valued having a sense of community which the inner-city parents lacked. As parents acknowledged in several locations: 'being a village community, we help each other out'.

INCOME

There was unanimous agreement that income made no difference to parents' capacity to love and value their children, but several groups and individuals acknowledged that the link between material and emotional care was strong. They stated that freedom from financial worries helped parents to be calm, patient and devote more attention to their children's emotional needs while having a car opened up recreational and educational opportunities by means of family outings and participation in activities outwith the local area.

Most important, having a reasonable family income enabled children to keep up with their peers in terms of dress and lifestyle, and several parents thought that facilitating this was part of good parenting. In this respect family income was thought directly to affect children's emotional well-being. The link between income and diet also affected children's physical health.

There was acknowledgement from high- and low-income parents that having too much money could also be problematic, in that children might fail to learn the value of money and become accustomed to a standard of life which might not be sustainable in adult life. Several parents whose income was derived from state benefits thought that explaining to children that they had to save up for major expenses such as Christmas brought the family closer together and helped make the children more responsible.

Parents who worked excessive hours in order to make a lot of money were not necessarily seen to be acting in the best interests of their family. The ideal was to reach an appropriate balance between working to increase one's standard of living while still having 'quality time' with the children.

TELEVISION

Television is one medium through which the outside world enters directly into the home. Although most parents thought their views on how to be a good parents were based on personal experience rather than messages in the media, they gave numerous examples of how television impacted on family life.

Television was seen as a powerful influence on children. Advertising fuelled demands for toys and introduced role models whose style of clothing children wanted to copy. Through story lines in children's programmes they were given a glimpse of life in different cultures and social situations, and some learned about such topics as teenage pregnancy and children's rights. One rural parent regretted that nearly all children's series were based in cities so that their own children's way of life was not reflected.

Several parents commented that television could introduce children to difficult subjects before they were able to understand them. News items showing children suffering, discussing homosexuality or dealing with rape forced parents into discussions they sometimes considered inappropriate or premature. On the positive side, television documentaries could helpfully open up and inform discussion on sensitive subjects such as illegal drugs and safe sex.

Only a few parents talked about controlling their children's use of television. One set of parents changed channels when any 'romantic' or violent scenes came on and a few other parents talked about turning the television off at certain time to encourage discussion. One parent worried that soap operas gave her daughter a false impression that casual sex was 'normal' but she chose to talk with her about this rather than ban the programmes. There is evidence that children themselves are selective in what they watch (Buckingham 1993).

Television and newspapers were the main means through which parents learned about children being abducted, harmed or killed, which fuelled their concerns about safety. Some drew children's attention to such stories to increase their awareness of potential risks. There was a view that these events were reported in such a way as to imply parents had been negligent and so encouraged parents to worry and be over protective.

Summary

Parenting children in middle childhood emerged as a multi-faceted task which took place in very different forms and types of families. Parents were subject to many influences within and outwith the family which impacted in different ways, reflecting parents' personalities as well as inner and material resources. There were many sources of stress which made it more difficult to be the calm, communicative parent most aspired to become.

Children on parents in middle childhood

The two studies provided opportunities for primary school-aged children to present their views about what being a parent entailed. The children who took part in the Parenting study were specifically asked about parenting, while those interviewed in the Well-being study spontaneously talked about parents and family life in response to questions about their own lives. On the whole children talked about their parents positively, as helpful people who cared about them. However, parents could also generate negative feelings and in some groups the reasons for this were discussed at length. In general, children did not think their parents were uncaring but that they were under a lot of pressure and had limited time and energy to devote to being a parent. These aspects are considered more fully in Chapter 7 which focuses on well-being, stress and support within the family. Here we outline briefly the key elements of children's perceptions of their parents.

How parents care for children

The children interviewed for both studies presented a common view of what children needed from parents. These could be categorised as being:

- cared for physically
- cared for emotionally by being listened to, taken seriously and valued
- prepared for adult life, for example by being taught right from wrong and not 'spoiled'.

In the same way that parents talked of caring for the 'whole' child, children recognised that physical care was a sign of love and valuing just as much as verbal support or taking time to talk. The preparation by parents of favourite and comforting foods was occasionally mentioned when children talked about being ill. Children spoke about the special care and attention they received from parents and sometimes they associated illness with particular foods (e.g. soup). Being encouraged to drink milk and eat fruit as well as being given favourite meals on special occasions (e.g. birthdays) were all viewed by children as expressions of parental love.

Children gave many examples of how meal times and preparing food were central to family life. Who did the cooking provided a good insight into how tasks were allocated within the family. In most families, mothers were primarily responsible for the cooking, but in some this was described as a shared task, often when both parents were working or when the father was unemployed. A few men had developed a reputation for preparing exotic meals for special occasions, for example curries, but as one girl commented: 'he leaves a mess. Mum has to go in and tidy up.' Some children also indicated that they themselves took a turn at preparing the evening meal or helping one or other parent.

A number of children described occasions when they had taken the opportunity to talk to their parents while they were making the tea. This was presumably a time when parents' presence could be relied on, when they were often alone and when reaction to difficult subjects could be tested. It was easier to chat while peeling the potatoes than to sit down for a 'heavy session'.

However, children were also aware that parents could find their demands irritating when they were preparing food. One girl drew a picture of her mother cooking the dinner, with a thought balloon above her head portraying that she wished to strangle her daughter who was chatting at her side. This unwittingly corresponded with the image of daughters talking non-stop which some parents also conjured up. Another child described how her mother could become irritated with her and her brother's behaviour when she was preparing food. She also was aware that it was a time when, if she repeatedly asked for something, her mother would usually give in to pressure.

Parents who readily succumbed to pressure were, however, not universally admired. Children applauded parents who limited the amount of sweets or possessions their children were allowed to have, either because too much of the wrong food might damage their health or because they might become 'spoiled' and selfish. At this stage, most children seemed still to accept the received wisdom of their parents, though some tested them constantly; most were prepared to accept parental rules, as long as they thought they were fair.

The pros and cons of parents

As children in the Well-being study talked about what made them happy or sad, discussion often centred on parents and family life. Many talked with relish about enjoying family outings and special occasions such as birthdays, holidays and Christmas. On the other hand, parental actions which were seen as unfair could be a cause of upset, for example being blamed for the actions of brothers and sisters. Some were unhappy when restrictions were imposed such as being 'grounded', or 'not allowed up the park', while others disliked being taken against their wishes to activities such as 'Anchor Boys'. A number of children said that just knowing they had acted against their parents' wishes could make them sad and to this was sometimes added anxiety about being deceptive or found out. Occasionally children referred to being left alone at home and several mentioned being unhappy when their parents argued.

Concerns about parental arguments were quite common, even when these might not be considered significant from the adult point of view. The prevalence of separation and divorce has created a climate where this is a real fear for children who worry that arguments are a sign of serious discord. However at least one child we spoke with was able to recognise some advantages from parental separation, while also giving an example of how parents can be valued without being daily present:

> My mum and dad are separated as well and every Tuesday and every Saturday she takes us out ... She does more things with us now than if she lived at home with us.

This comment was made by a nine-year-old boy in the course of a discussion about lack of parental time. This topic arose in many groups. Though several children felt they could rely on their parents to be available when needed, others found that parents were often too busy and preoccupied. Most children were confident that their parents cared about them and recognised that much parental activity was to do with earning a living to provide for them, but they nevertheless regretted that time was so limited. Indeed for many this was their main complaint.

Another common theme was that parents did not always understand how various situations or problems affected children. Again most children were confident that their parents were keen to act in their best interests, but felt that they tended to see things from their own adult perspective, rather than the child's. As a result, parents sometimes dismissed as insignificant worries which caused children considerable distress. Rows with friends or worries about warring parents were two sources of anxiety which some parents were thought to underestimate. We return to these themes and explore them more fully in Chapter 7.

Parents under stress

Just as many parents thought middle childhood was a difficult time for their children, so children thought life was tough for the parents. They were aware that parents worried about them, primarily about their education and their safety, and that they also had worries of their own, mainly about money and work:

> Adults are worried all the time, because of their children at school, and getting a good education.

> My dad worries a lot ... he worries if something is not going very well, and he can't do it — my dad worries — so does my mum — say you told him something

and he doesn't know what to do — my dad worries as well — ... when my dad worries he gets stressed out and then he gets quite moody ... — my mum worries about bills.

Some groups expressed the view that parents were more stressed than children, because they had more serious concerns, 'for example about money and work'. Others commented that adults, unlike children, were not able to get help from other people. They were the adults and had to sort things out. Thus, at least two messages about being an adult had been absorbed: work and money are important concerns and you have to cope on your own.

Conclusion

Children's expectations of parents mostly corresponded to the tasks identified by parents themselves and they identified a wide range of parental actions which made them feel cared for. When parents were found wanting, this was usually explained in terms of them being overworked or under pressure, rather then uncaring. Children did not expect their parents to be perfect and were predisposed to making allowances.

Parents and children were in agreement that time was an essential ingredient in parenting at this stage, and that it was a commodity which was often in short supply. A study by Gibbons et al. (cited in Department of Health 1995) also reported that children wanted parents to spend time with them, though another British study indicated that control over time and space was a central concern for primary-aged children, most of whom experienced more opportunities for this at home than at school (Mayall 1994b). This and children's competing wishes to be independent yet cared for, would suggest that individual children's needs will best be met through open communication and negotiation between children and parents. The subsequent chapters give an impression of how children and parents manage key aspects of their lives during these critical middle years.

CHAPTER 4

Whose Life is it Anyway?

Care and control in middle childhood

Introduction

Having set the scene from both parents' and children's perspectives, we now turn to consider in more detail some key dimensions of their lives. Parents devoted much time to discussing the various ways in which their relationship with their children changed during middle childhood and a key aspect of this was how best to manage children's growing independence and autonomy. The trick was to find the correct balance between continuing to provide as much care and guidance as was needed, while allowing enough space for children to make decisions, take increasing responsibility for themselves and so develop as individuals in their own right. In addition parents had to find ways of persuading or coercing their children to adhere to the limits they set.

In practice, the shift towards autonomy was effected through decisions on such everyday issues as the age at which children were allowed to go out on their own, whether they chose their own food or clothes and the extent to which they were consulted about decisions affecting the family. Unsurprisingly, there were differing perspectives on how such decisions or rules should be made and that illusive 'point of balance' varied, depending on the issue. Parents generally were keener to regulate the amount of freedom their children had outwith the home than to determine what they wore or ate. Strategies in relation to specific issues such as safety and diet are outlined in subsequent chapters on these topics. Here we consider some of the factors which shaped parents' views and outline their general approach to discipline.

The social context

Virtually all the parents we met with were white and Scottish, so that their views reflected attitudes to children within that culture. As Solberg (1990) pointed out, cultural and social factors create the context within which individual families construct ideas about appropriate levels of autonomy in childhood. Solberg's survey of Norwegian parents found they were quite content to leave their ten-year-old children on their own at the end of the school day. The children themselves had been active in bringing about this attitude by gradually making less use of the after-school care which had previously been arranged for them. Thus, the way in which childhood was reconceptualised as comprising more freedom and self-care for children had been a subtle process of negotiation between parents and their children within the context of increased maternal employment. Moreover, the resulting arrangements were probably more acceptable to Norwegian than UK parents, in part because Norway is less urbanised.

From our discussions with Scottish parents, it was not evident that increasing employment of mothers was leading to less parental supervision at an earlier stage. Rather the current social climate seems to be encouraging parents to restrict children's freedom more than in the past. Parents indicated that media reports of children having been harmed by strangers raised their anxiety, while at the same time often implying that lack of appropriate parental supervision was to blame.

Parents' behaviour also tends to be scrutinised when children commit crimes such as joy-riding, stealing or using drugs. Alongside shock about the murder of Jamie Bulger by two ten-year-old boys, fears were expressed that parents were failing to provide appropriate guidance and supervision. The imposition of curfews (e.g. in Lanarkshire in 1997) and moves to make parents responsible for their children's behaviour at school create a climate in which continuing parental control is encouraged, while media campaigns urge parents to be vigilant, knowing where their children are, what they are doing and who they are with.

Alongside this growing concern about supervision, with the implication that greater control should be exercised over children, from another direction growing attention has been given to children's rights, which are often thought to entail fewer restrictions on children. Britain is committed to implementing the provisions of the UN Convention on the Rights of the Child and the children's legislation which now governs each part of the United Kingdom incorporates its basic tenets (Tisdall 1997). As we report in more detail in Chapter 9, few parents were well-informed about these developments but they had absorbed the message that children's views should be taken into account when making decisions which affect them and that methods of control or discipline should not infringe basic human rights.

It is evident then that the social context incorporates contradictory messages about how and at what pace parents should respond to their children's need and wishes for increasing autonomy. We were interested in what parents themselves had to say.

Negotiation and control

Most of the parents felt they continued to have a fair amount of influence over their children and believed it was very much in their children's best interests that this was so. Most thought that children needed a lot of guidance and that it was sometimes the parents' duty to insist on the safest or most beneficial course of action. However they also repeatedly acknowledged that as children approached the teenage years, parents could no longer lay down the law and expect it to be obeyed. They had to learn to negotiate or, as some parents said, 'to manipulate' their children:

> I think there's a lot of compromise and manipulation — Aye, but you get that either from the parents or the kids, the kids are great at doing that — We've got to do it but in manner that, no so much you're manipulating them, you're just sort of… — Oh aye, I've got to manipulate E into doing things but in a roundabout manner know what I mean without being too obvious and saying to him, 'look for God's sake get that done', I've got to put it across and make him think that he's doing it to help me as opposed to telling him what to do, you've got to manipulate.

Of course, *negotiation* and *manipulation* are not the same. Negotiation implies a willingness to share power and take account of the other person's point if view, while manipulation involved retaining control by devious means. Each parent's approach inevitably reflected the relationship with and view of their child but both negotiation and manipulation were in the repertoire of most parents.

Despite different parental practices, most parents expressed the view that negotiation was the *preferred* method. It was acknowledged that a more autocratic stance was sometimes necessary, but this was then justified by reference to the nature of the child, the parent or other circumstances. It could be that children were seen as particularly wilful/disobedient and requiring firm handling, or the parents acknowledged that they themselves had no patience for negotiation, either innately or because they were over-stressed. In two-parent households, one parent sometimes set firm rules, while the other was more open to compromise – a 'good and bad cop' routine, as one father called it. There was a belief that it was more usual for fathers to take on the strict role but several parents indicated the mothers were the strict ones in their families. Several women referred to themselves as the more authoritarian parent who was more likely to adhere firmly to rules and carry out promised punishments. While some of these mothers valued their husbands' patience, other saw them as easily manipulated.

Whatever their approach, virtually everyone expected good parents to be in control. Flexibility and consistency were both valued, a position reconciled by agreeing that consistency meant having clear fixed boundaries within which there might be some leeway. An example was having a rule that children would only eat sweets at weekends but occasionally relaxing this if there was a special occasion mid-week. The power of the parent was implicit in that they may or may not grant an exception to the rule. There was also recognition that parents' changing moods made complete consistency impossible but it was still seen as an ideal to aim for. Having to adjust to parents' moods was seen as an inevitable part of childhood and some parents favoured acknowledging this and letting children know when parents felt under stress.

Approaches to negotiation and control were thus influenced by a number of factors, some pertaining to society in general and others to the family. At a family or individual level, how parents handed over control was shaped to a considerable extent by general parenting style, children's behaviour and parents' perceptions of the children and their status within the family.

Parenting style

A number of mainly American writers have reviewed research on parenting styles and noted associations with different outcomes for children (e.g. Maccoby and Martin 1983). It has been concluded that an 'authoritative' style combining emotional warmth and firm but flexible discipline is associated with the 'best' outcomes in that the children tend to be happy, active, compliant and conscientious. Permissive, overprotective and authoritarian styles are more likely to promote passivity, aggression or defiance. Evidently such conclusions are highly generalised and include more than a dash of value judgement about what is desirable.

Research into the emotional effects of parental abuse on children has concluded that the most harmful combination is for children to be consistently exposed to high criticism, while being shown little warmth (DoH 1995). Occasional smacking or harsh discipline causes less emotional trauma if it occurs within a context of parental care, while children who feel unloved are less resilient to such treatment.

Lax or sporadically harsh discipline in early and middle childhood has long been identified as a predictor of juvenile crime (Loughran 1995). Laybourn (1986) compared patterns of supervision of boys from ten years onwards in poor neighbourhoods. She found that some parents held their children accountable, expected them to do more at home and acted quickly if they were worried about peer associations. Others had few rules and did little checking on how the youngsters were spending their time. The latter's children were much more likely to be in trouble at school or with the law.

Although all the parents we met set limits, they approached this in very different ways. Some parents were predisposed to set absolute rather than negotiated rules and to be concerned with sanctions rather than family agreements. This to some extent reflected whether children were seen as inherently naughty and requiring close control or basically good and competent enough to negotiate. However some parents were natural autocrats and, although they saw the value of a more democratic approach, felt they lacked the patience or skill to put this into practice.

Children's behaviour

While the parents' approach would undoubtedly help shape their offsprings' expectations and behaviour, children were by no means passive recipients of parental decisions. From about the age of eight children were seen as more able to present their points of view and to influence parents' decisions, not only by arguing their case but by the type of children they were. Some parents with more than one child had found themselves making quite different decisions about what children of the same age were expected or allowed to do, attributing this to gender, position in the family or the child's personality (compliant or challenging).

> I think the demands of the child [affect the level of freedom allowed]. My oldest child was not adventurous by nature and she was quite happy to accept what time limit I gave to her, but he's a far more adventurous person and willing to take risks, and it has to be taken into account. He wants to stretch himself.

From their individual experience, this parent and others thus confirmed the widely accepted view that beliefs and behaviour within the family are not simply imposed by parents but are developed and modified through complex communications amongst parents and children (Dallos 1995). Another study concerning children on the threshold of adolescence emphasised the importance of the different ways in which rules are negotiated in relation to domestic behaviour and interaction, appearance and privacy, and peer leisure activities (du Bois-Raymond, Buchner and Kruger 1993).

Parents' perceptions of the child and their status within the family

Parents' reactions to children acting autonomously were influenced not only by the nature of the child's behaviour but also by how this was interpreted by parents. To some parents, a child's ability to argue a case strongly was evidence of potential leadership, while to others it was insolence. Research carried out in the 1960s and 70s indicated that more middle-class parents were inclined to promote autonomy while more working-class children were encouraged to be obedient and conforming (Kohn 1969; Newson and Newson 1963, 1970, 1976). There was no obvious way in which class seemed to affect the approach of the parents who took part in our research. More significant seemed to be how parents' viewed their children's status in relation to themselves.

Whether children were seen as inferior, equal or superior in relation to their parents represented an important dimension of parental perceptions. Some parents based their attitudes on their perceptions of the child's competence, while others were mindful of their own power, sometimes perceived in economic terms: since parents paid the bills they could call the tune.

Status could of course vary in different aspects of life. Children might be seen as more intelligent than their parents but lacking experience of life and so inferior to parents in terms of ability to understand and make decisions. A few parents described children as having superior understanding of their own needs and feelings which parents had to strive to understand and respond to appropriately. Some parents, mostly single parents or parents of single children, thought of the relationship with their children as akin to an equal partnership, though the parents' authority was still recognised:

> It is something where she asserts herself as being an equal partner. Sometimes she asks me so perhaps it is not quite as equal a partnership as she might want it to be.

In contrast, other parents disliked when their children made a bid to be treated as equal or even superior and resisted this:

> They try to become their own person. They realise that they need their space and they start to speak to you as if you're their equal. And the funny thing about it is, you start to speak to them as if you're their equal. You have to stop and think, Wait a minute! Who's the adult here and who's the child? I'm reacting with this child as if I'm child! I shouldn't have to do this. I should be able to stand back and say, No, because I say so, and that's the end of it!

> They see they themselves getting big so they think, hey I'm big, I'm an adult, I'm the boss now and I can do it. So in their minds they think they can tell you — See my oldest one, he's the same, 'I'm the boss, cause I'm the oldest now and my da's no here so I'm the boss' — See what I mean, I've had that a couple of times.

In these ways parents illustrated how fluid and varied are the boundaries between childhood and adulthood (Qvortrup *et al.* 1994).

Discipline in practice

Quite a number of parents said that their children were not seriously disobedient at all or that only a 'look' or knowledge of their parents' disapproval was needed to 'bring them back into line'. These parents were not necessarily less controlling than others. Since their children's behaviour corresponded with their own expectations, there was little need for discipline as such.

Nevertheless, many instances were mentioned of children doing things their parents disapproved of and wanted to stop. There were acts of commission (with victims) and omission (with presumed negative long-term consequences for the children themselves). These included being cheeky to adults, not washing or brushing teeth, not tidying their rooms or helping at home, as well as more extreme behaviour such as fighting and fire raising.

According to parents, their main responses to bad behaviour were:

- explanation/discussion
- 'giving a row'
- removing toys and other cherished items, e.g. computer
- not allowing to watch TV
- 'grounding'
- shouting
- smacking
- reporting to someone else (the other parent, school staff, or police).

Usually these actions appeared to be specific though often routinised responses to particular behaviour by individual children, but a few parents described more general strategies. One father described how he and his wife arranged a day out to provide an opportunity to discuss with their daughters the increase in fighting and arguing within the home. By the end of the day they had agreed rules of conduct which involved each party withdrawing for a few minutes and thinking rather than reacting immediately in anger. Another father explained that his family had held regular family meetings since their children were about eight years old. Each child was asked for 'agenda items' and encouraged to discuss anything which was worrying them. This allowed rules to be reviewed and any concerns to be aired. Although there was an apparent democracy about these meetings in that children could challenge parents, it was also clear that parents remained in control. The mother in the second family also made use of behaviour charts if there was a specific problem with either of her two children. She was a teacher and this was one of several examples of drawing on professional skills and knowledge in the parenting sphere.

Many of the parents acknowledged that they had smacked their children. The majority thought that corporal punishment was acceptable and reasonably effective with younger children, but that by the eight to twelve stage it became generally ineffective. The following quotes express the views of many parents:

> Hitting doesn't really do any good, not at that age anyway it doesn't. I've got one that's five, I skelp him and that's it. I skelp him on the backside and that's it, he's going to do what he's told. But when they're older, no.

> I don't think a smack would work now anyway. I think if you have to smack a nine-, ten- or eleven-year-old there's a problem. You should be able to sit down and talk to them. I don't think smacking is the answer.

Reasoning was seen as more appropriate than a behavioural approach when children were old enough to understand why their behaviour was dangerous or wrong. However, even if they would seldom resort to smacking, the majority of parents were keen to retain the threat in the background. Only a minority of parents saw smacking as wrong in itself, despite recent campaigns to have it legally banned, as in certain other European countries (Newell 1995).

In practical terms, finding an alternative to smacking was not always easy. A group of married mothers from the suburban area pointed out that parents had been told not to smack but been given no alternative strategies. Virtually every parent agreed that they would prefer to talk things over and reach agreement with their children but some found it difficult to put this into practice. This applied to some of the mothers from one of the city schemes:

> I've tried everything, my oldest one he just doesn't say anything just ignores you and that makes me really angry, I think 'cause he sees it makes me really mad. I'll say I'm talking to you. Don't you dare ignore me, know what I mean. I think sometimes 'that's ridiculous shouting at your kids' ... — I just shout 'cause I don't want to hit them — That's like me.

The mothers quoted above were at a loss to know how to manage their children more effectively. Withdrawing privileges seemed as ineffective as smacking and they felt powerless and worried that things were going so wrong. One child frequently started fires and others were described as insolent and out of control. They said they would love to be able to get their children's cooperation by talking but did not see this as a possibility for themselves, only for people who had less stress in their life and so had more time and energy.

Some of the adoptive parents we met with spoke of their children's significant emotional and behavioural difficulties, thought to be the result of foetal alcohol syndrome or abuse in their early years. The children's behaviour was characterised by constant control battles and several parents had adopted a particular approach to parenting developed by members of the Attachment Disorder Parents' Network – Parent Assertiveness using Consequences with Empathy, or PACE. The term 'attachment disorder' has become a prominent way of making sense of relationship and behaviour difficulties in the adoption field (Archer 1996; Howe 1995b).

According to the PACE model, parents allow children to retain as much control as possible and to learn from the consequences of their behaviour. This might sometimes result in parents taking no action to prevent a child suffering, by for example allowing a child to go out wearing no coat and feel cold, rather than have a battle about what he or she should wear. It takes some skill and forethought to operate this system, but discovering an approach which worked for them had been an empowering experience for these parents. Some thought that the basic methods would be helpful for many parents.

Children's views on care and control

None of the children we met were asked specifically about the ways in which their parents controlled or disciplined them but numerous spontaneous references to this topic were made, some of which were reported in Chapter 2 when outlining children's views of parents.

In general children indicated that parental care and control were not usually in conflict. At this age most children expected and accepted that parents would make rules and would discipline them if they did wrong. Being smacked or 'grounded' made them sad but they only complained about this if the punishment was seen as unjustified or unfair. Harsh words could however be very hurtful, making children feel unworthy and unloved.

The disciplining of other children who bullied or misbehaved was also welcomed. Children derived some reassurance from the fact that adults were in charge and approved of teachers and parents who could be relied on to punish bad behaviour.

Perhaps surprisingly, children made few complaints about being overprotected or too closely supervised. Although many parents told us that children argued continually for more freedom, in the interview situation parental restrictions were usually reported as if they were self-evidently appropriate and there was almost a sense of pride that their parents took care to protect them. In contrast, the teenagers surveyed by Gordon and Grant (1997) were much more inclined to challenge parental authority and see rules as unreasonable. Other studies of adolescence have indicated that, though certain specific rules for example about clothes are resented or challenged, most teenagers accept parental authority and value parental guidance when making major decisions (Coleman and Hendry 1990; Noller and Callan 1991). It seems to be the case that global authority and boundary setting is wanted, but certain specific rules in some domains (like clothes) are resented or challenged.

Despite the younger children's apparent acceptance of parental restrictions, parents' beliefs about the value of being given enough freedom to develop as an individual was borne out. A number of children said that being given more freedom and autonomy made them feel good about themselves and opened up opportunities for more varied leisure activities.

Summary and conclusion

Many parents spoke about how to give children increasing autonomy, while continuing to provide adequate guidance and control. Modern parents receive confusing and sometimes contradictory messages about the extent to which they should give children freedom to make mistakes and the approach of individual parents seemed to reflect a range of influences including parenting style, the children's behaviour and personality and how these were perceived by their parents. A range of strategies were used to discipline children and influence their behaviour. Though negotiation and discussion were considered preferable, parents also resorted to more autocratic methods. In the interviews children seemed willing to accept parents' restrictions, though parents reported much testing of boundaries at home.

It might be argued that balancing care and control is a challenge for parents throughout childhood, not only during the middle years. There are however some distinctive features as children approach adolescence. Though still inexperienced and vulnerable enough to need parental supervision and guidance, children of this age are becoming competent enough to manage much of their day away from their parents, so that there is increased scope for doing without parental control or resisting it. Believing that their control over their children is beginning to lessen, parents to some extent view this stage as a last chance to influence them before the critical move to secondary school when the influence of the outside world and peers in particular is expected to increase. However, during middle childhood parents still feel very much responsible for their children. Whereas there is recognition that teenagers can be a law unto themselves, at this stage parents are supposed to be in charge. Thus it is seen as a reflection on parental competence if children are out every night, are too tired to work well at school or come to grief in a risky situation.

Parental controls were mostly prompted by concern for children's best interests, whether to teach appropriate behaviour and values or to keep safe from physical harm. Safety was a major concern which significantly shaped parents' behaviour and outlook.

CHAPTER 5

Safety and Danger

Introduction

In recent years the high profile media coverage given to incidents of child abduction, sexual abuse, and murder by strangers have created among parents a climate of fear and apprehension of the outside world (McNeish and Roberts 1995; Roberts, Smith and Bryce 1995). Such incidents are extremely rare, and are not thought to have increased in frequency over the past, but the increased attention given to them brings them nearer home and makes them appear more common than they really are. In addition, campaigns designed to warn children to say 'No' to strangers and drugs have probably inadvertently contributed to the feeling parents have that the world outside the home is a dangerous place, full of threats against which children need to be continually guarded. More recently, there has been increased awareness that in their efforts to protect children against the cruel world, parents are in fact curtailing their children's activities to such an extent that their quality of life and development are being impaired (Adams 1995).

The majority of parents we interviewed, irrespective of area, expressed real fears about their children's safety and viewed dangers in the social and physical environment as a major threat to their well-being. In the self-completion forms, 'safety' (from strangers, sexual abuse and traffic) was the most frequently voiced parental concern, followed by 'drug abuse'. The outside world was seen as dangerous, and several parents talked about the stress of constantly worrying whether their children would be safe when they were outwith the home. The following quote was typical of many:

> I think probably the biggest stress is worrying about their safety, because they think they are so independent. They're independent in the home and they think they're independent outside the home too and that nothing can happen to them. And every paper you pick up, and every news report on the television tells you

about the terrible things that happen to children. You worry about that all the time.

This mother's distinction between the safety of the home where children were competent and the dangers of the outside world where they were vulnerable was a common theme. Hence parents found the eight to twelve stage an anxious time since children increasingly wished to spend time outside the home. For the most part parents recognised that children at this stage should be more independent than younger ones, yet did not see their children as able to fend for themselves like adults or even adolescents.

Hazards and dangers perceived by parents

The most common and apparently most intense worry among parents was that their children would be abducted or sexually abused by a stranger. Although people were aware that the numbers of children involved in such incidents was very small, they were not prepared to take the chance that their child would become one of them. The risk was low but the potential damage devastating. In addition to being influenced by media reports, local events fuelled parents' fears that 'it could happen here'.

> I don't know whether it was just a tall story or not but one of the girls in the house just next door ... a couple of years ago she said that somebody stopped in a van up at the shops and was trying to tempt her. I think the police were all involved in that. It brought it home to you. That's one of your neighbours and it stays with you. I think you have to hear of somebody nearby for it really to make a difference to you. Because up until then you think, well, it happens away in the south of England, and it happens away in the north of Scotland, but it doesn't happen here on my own doorstep. And when you hear about it, it makes you think differently.

Parents who lived in the comparatively 'safe' suburban and rural areas expressed many fears about 'stranger danger'. For rural parents the safety of the home domain extended to the village where there was a sense of security because everyone knew everyone else. Children were warned to be wary of 'outsiders' but there was an assumption that village people could be trusted, and children were given freedom to roam within these bounds. In the suburban areas by contrast it was believed that even local people might constitute a threat, so parents were more vigilant about their own neighbourhoods.

In contrast to these largely hypothetical fears of abduction by unknown strangers, parents in the city schemes were more concerned about the immediate dangers to their children of harassment by specific known individuals or groups in their local area, of which many had direct experience. Their main worries were about local youths and neighbours who were aggressive or misused alcohol and/or drugs. They worried that these people would harm their children, steal from them or encourage them to use drugs or alcohol. Parents were also concerned that children could be bullied by other local children when out playing. (We discuss bullying at school in Chapter 8.)

We have presented a gloomy account of parents feeling beleaguered within their own homes. However, though this was the majority view, not all parents shared these fears of the outside world. One or two recognised the prevailing anxiety and called for parents to take a more balanced view:

> There just seems to be a collective anxiety, you know, that everybody's waiting for something to go wrong and the actual likelihood of anything going wrong is very small. I think we need to get it back into perspective ... They all seem to be worried about is their child going to get run over, is their child going to go with a stranger, is their child going to get into drugs?

Although all parents were concerned about safety, the nature of their concerns and the steps taken to reduce risks reflected the geographical area in which families were living. There was a strong perception, held by country and city dwellers alike, that rural areas were safer than cities. It was also commonly accepted that girls' freedom was restricted more than boys. This was commonly explained in terms of fears of sexual abuse, though several parents recalled that girls had always been more closely controlled than boys, even before awareness of sexual assault was high. The parents seemed largely unaware that a considerable percentage of victims of sexual abuse are boys.

Parental strategies for keeping children safe

All parents worried about safety and they adopted a range of strategies to promote it. They identified a range of three broad approaches:

1. close supervision accompanied by high curtailment of freedom
2. increased freedom accompanied by high investment in preparation and equipping children to cope
3. considerable freedom combined with minimal preparation or supervision.

These three possible approaches are in line with those found in other studies (Laybourn 1986). The parents we interviewed indicated that they used the first or second approach, or a combination of the two. While several described other parents they knew who followed the third approach, this was considered irresponsible and none of the parents we met said they adopted it.

Supervision

This first approach was to supervise children as closely as possible. In response to the dangers in their area, this was a favoured strategy for many parents in the city scheme. Some did not allow their children to play outside at all. Others only allowed them to do so if they were directly under the eye of a responsible adult or within specified boundaries:

> In this area, no, there's just no way I'm letting my boy out. I know, as I say he does get out sometimes, but my mum stays round the corner and she watches him constantly. He never gets round to this bit 'cause it's too busy with cars. It's also to do with some of the young parents who have moved in and I don't know, they don't wash the stairs, they don't keep their pathways clean.

One mother insisted that her neighbours allow her son to play football near his home where she could supervise him. Another said she spent the whole of the summer break watching her children play.

This close monitoring of children's activities allowed parents in the city scheme to take direct action when their children were threatened by other children or adults. Against this had to be balanced the need to retain reasonably friendly relationships with neighbours, recognising that children had to live among them. Challenging neighbours was quite often left to mothers because they were seen as better at negotiating, whereas if fathers became involved it was more likely to escalate into a physical fight. Some situations were just too risky for action:

> My D, he got chased by boys with knives — My other boy got hit with a baseball bat, but you couldn't go to the parents' door 'cause they were all junkies. No way I'm going to somebody's door with an Alsatian like that, and I'm there to moan about their son!

In contrast, parents in the safer suburban areas laid less emphasis on supervising play. Though many insisted on accompanying their children to and from school, there was some recognition that this might be seen as overprotective:

> You see parent after parent coming to collect even primary 7s — Well my daughter's primary 7. What I let her do now is she gets on the bus and gets down the road and she is met at the bus stop by myself or my husband or my mother-in-law. It's ridiculous, she is 5 feet 4 and looks 15 and you think 'good gracious'.

Parents in the city scheme were usually well aware of the drawbacks of curtailing children's freedom and many of them regretted that their children could not experience the carefree times they cherished in recalling their own childhoods. Despite the fact that children nowadays usually have far more material possessions, there was general agreement that the quality of life for children has not improved. As one mother put it:

> Although you're maybe buying them more toys and they want the Reebok trainers and you're buying them things like that, they've no got a better life cause you're too feart, you don't let them go anywhere or do anything … you don't let them live.

Where children were not allowed out to play at all, parents spoke of a number of specific problems that arose as a result. Some felt obliged to buy expensive computer games to occupy children indoors. Children got no exercise. 'Grounding' was lost as a possible sanction; one parent spoke of inventing misdemeanours to have an excuse to keep the child in. Family life became more tense and fraught since parents did not get a break, and the balance of authority within the home could shift if the child was given additional power within the home to compensate for not getting out to play, for example having choice over which TV programmes should be watched. Thus actions to keep children safe put considerable pressure on families and had a significant impact on how they operated.

Preparation

In the second approach, preferred by most families in suburban and rural areas, parents attempted to allow their children the increasing freedom they craved, relying for safety on teaching their child how to protect themselves and cope with situations that might arise. It was recognised that this involves a degree of residual anxiety, which parents have to live with. One mother provides a good example of this second approach, clearly identifying that she based her actions on her eleven-year-old daughter's individual needs and wishes rather than her own fears.

> I think you've got to be really objective about what you're doing with your child, you know, it's really to stand outside of it and say, Well wait a minute. What are they capable of doing? Am I underestimating them? … You're drawing on their willingness to take, accept responsibility for it, I think, and they're different, they're all different.

This approach requires parents to trust their (prepared) child's judgement. A few mothers commented that their children knew their own social world better than the parents did and were more able to gauge when and where they would be at risk. One mother, for example, described how her daughter had elected not to stay the night with a friend, because she felt uncomfortable in her house.

Keeping children safe while allowing them freedom essentially involved managing their links with the outside world. Depending on their basic conceptions of children's capabilities and needs, parents adopted a range of strategies to do this. Virtually all parents in all areas gave their children repeated warnings and drew their attention to newspaper articles or television programmes to bring home the fact that other children had been harmed. One parent felt that you had to 'terrify' your children nowadays to ensure they were adequately aware of the dangers.

However, additionally, many parents relied more heavily on teaching their children 'survival skills'. These included:

- having an agreed code word which any stranger collecting the child on the parents' behalf would know

- working out strategies for dealing with difficult situations (e.g. having your money stolen)

- helping children develop their own sense of what is safe

- encouraging children to be assertive and to challenge anyone who made them feel uncomfortable

- encouraging children to learn self defence, e.g. through learning karate

- advising children on how to handle bullies.

These strategies thus aimed to equip children to be able to defend themselves and make the environment more safe by influencing the behaviour of other people. The degree of thought and detailed preparation that parents put into teaching their children to cope was striking:

> What I generally do is, if she's going some place for the first time I'll go with her there the first time, take her back, so that she knows the buses, knows where she's going, and then after that she picks it up from there. If she was insecure I would go again.

A group of parents from the suburban school talked about how they decided whether an activity or event was safe or not. They described a progression with certain age-related thresholds of permitted acts; for example after you are in secondary school you can go into town on your own without adult supervision. Going into town with friends was seen as a landmark in itself. Parents relied partly on logic and partly on intuition. They had to feel comfortable with the level of safety and risk, which was the product of a number of factors, for example the parents' familiarity with where the child was going, who they were going with, whether other parents thought it was acceptable. For each threshold there could be sub-stages. One example given was that of a child being allowed for the first time to go into town alone. She was allowed to make the outward journey with friends, but the parent insisted on meeting them in town to drive them home.

Efforts to teach children survival skills were not confined to suburban parents. They were equally important for many parents in the city scheme. However, in these areas the focus was different, relating to actual harassment and bullying by local people rather than the possibility of molestation by strangers. One mother described how she had taught her daughters to 'humour' rather than antagonise the drunk men who frequented their street. A number of parents described how they encouraged their children to 'hit back' other children who hit them first. They had little confidence that their children would survive in the area equipped solely with negotiating skills.

The children's perspective

The children in both our studies had a perspective on safety and danger that was, on the whole, markedly at odds with that of these parents. Safety, which was the prime concern of all parents, hardly figured in their discussions, and then mainly in response to prompting by us. With the exception of one group, which we refer to later, the risks posed by strangers, drugs or traffic were almost never mentioned as causes of fear or distress. In view of the publicity given to 'stranger danger' and the warnings all parents said they had given their children, the lack of any spontaneous reference to this was particularly striking. In general, children viewed adults with trust rather than suspicion (see Moran *et al.* 1997). They were far more concerned with other dangers, real or imaginary. Asked about 'feeling safe', they mentioned adults protecting them from bullies, injury, the dark, the elements, even ghosts, but none of them saw safety in terms of protection from other adults. Indeed, the following quote from a younger rural boy shows that he felt reassured precisely because a noise came from a person albeit a stranger (therefore safe) rather than a ghost:

> The most frightened I've ever felt was yesterday ... the old school, some people think it's haunted, and me and my friends were going through it, and we heard this noise ... I went running down and told my mum and dad ... my dad went to see ... and then my dad said there was no one there – it was [just] this man raking up leaves [picks up next card]. I felt really safe when my dad had said there was no one in the old school.

On only one issue did children's and parents' concerns coincide. Children from all areas confirmed that harassment and bullying by local residents is indeed a problem which worries them, though its nature was more serious in the city schemes:

> My mum and dad go out to the shops together with us 'cause there's gangs in our bit and people that steal — And they nearly smashed my window — ... My dad came along to the shops with us and he said my mum can't go out ... — We can't go out to play cos there's people that drink downstairs and they smash windows and that, like they are always out on the street starting fights and that — I can't go out sometimes cos they are fighting.

> One time we went over to the park, my brother J and I, we were on our bikes, and G my [older] brother was just walking the dog, and G went in the tennis court where these boys were playing, and the boys started swearing at G, and I gave J my bike, and I took the dog, and we were running away from them, 'cause they were chasing us. And I let my dog off the lead, and they got big stones, and they were throwing it at my dog ... and they were threatening me ...

> It was about a month ago, and we were getting bullied by these big boys, right, we were getting trapped — It was frightening — We were trapped in between two boys in the middle of [the road].

> One time a boy threw a banger at my jacket, down in a football place, we got it off, but it exploded. It was all right then, but it melted through, and my mum and dad went spare at the boys that were there.

Events like this were common in the city scheme, but apparently incidents were isolated elsewhere, though nonetheless frightening when they occurred. This suggests that parents in city schemes are well in tune with their children's concerns, and that the actions they take to protect them are valued. However the concentration of parents from other areas on the issue of stranger danger may be diverting them from recognising their children's own more immediate anxieties, and their need for protection and reassurance.

Safety in contrasting environments

The apparent divergence between parents' and children's perceptions of their localities was particularly noticeable in the contrast we found between the views of children and parents in the rural areas studied. There was a strong perception among rural parents (which was shared by city dwellers) that country areas were safer than cities. Yet the rural children in our Well-being sample (whose head teacher confirmed to us that the local environment was very safe for children to play and wander in since there was little traffic and strangers were rare), expressed more fears to us than children of any other group, including those from the city scheme. Some mentioned unpleasant encounters with tramps, drug addicts and neighbourhood bullies. Several had

had an unpleasant experience with a disagreeable neighbour, and some talked of fear at being left alone in the house. A group of older children expressed concerns about drugs, teenage pregnancies and stranger danger. They were the only children in the whole sample to raise these issues.

It seems on the face of it paradoxical that the children with the most openly expressed anxieties lived in the area which would seem to be the safest. However, the two may interconnect. Because rural environments are perceived by parents as safe (which in terms of criminal activity they are), children are subjected to fewer restrictions, and reduced chaperonage. They thus have a greater likelihood of encountering situations which, though not life threatening, are nonetheless unnerving.

> When my mum goes away and doesn't tell me she's going anywhere, if, like she's over the road and I don't know where she is, I really start to get worried … that she won't come back or something.

In contrast, because urban environments are regarded as risky, children are closely supervised and/or specifically given help in coping, and are therefore sheltered from the harsh realities to a large extent, feeling more secure as a result. The exception to this is in the city schemes where real threats exist, some of which defy parents' best efforts to protect their children from them.

This paradox also applies to differential protection of boys and girls. It is known that girls are given less freedom to roam than boys (Hillman 1993; Naylor 1986). Our parents confirmed this fact and explained it in terms of fears of sexual abuse. Yet boys are in fact statistically more at risk from injury and harm (Katz 1993), probably because of their greater freedom.

We have seen that urban parents fretted about the restrictions they placed on their children, and we know that, given the opportunity, children enjoy having independent mobility (Berg and Medrich 1980). However, none of our urban children voiced serious resentment of parental restrictions; possibly they were accepted as part of life or even evidence of caring.

Conclusion

Overall there was considerable discrepancy between the views of parents and children on safety and danger. Parents took a wider and long-term view of risks, and they may need to protect their children from dangers that the children are unaware of. However it is important that they are also sensitive to children's own immediate concerns. The gap in perceptions found in the two studies suggests that parents in all areas should be more alert to the immediate anxiety children experience in relation to bullying, harassment and being left alone in the house, and should keep the more remote risks of drug abuse, and particularly stranger danger, in proportion.

There may be a difficulty here. Many parents acknowledged intellectually that it was more likely that a child would be sexually abused by someone they knew rather than a stranger but this knowledge did not necessarily impact on their behaviour. They tended to make judgements about safety based on their own values, assuming for example that children would be safe among committed, good-living people at church groups and in sport, despite the fact that abuse has been uncovered and well publicised in both these domains. Only the relatively few parents whose knowledge of abuse was based on personal or professional experience talked about warning children that trusted people could pose a threat. It may be that messages about safety only influence behaviour if they are consistent with personal experience and values. Hence the majority of parents still believed (despite evidence to the contrary) that the outside world is the danger, and the home is the haven; just as the majority of children believed (despite repeated warnings) that adults are to be trusted.

CHAPTER 6

Physical Health

Introduction

There is agreement nowadays that health is not just the absence of disease but, in the words of the World Health Organisation, is a 'state of complete physical, mental and social well-being...' (Downie, Fyfe and Tannahill 1990). In part, this widened definition is due to the remarkable elimination and control over the past century of many of the fatal illnesses that were once thought part of life. Now that most children have been freed from major illness, we are able to aim for a childhood that is also free from major emotional and social stress.

Parents in our study clearly embraced this twofold notion, agreeing that a holistic perspective was needed, and that children's health involved emotional and psychological as well as physical well-being. Sometimes they differentiated between the two in terms of 'actual' or 'real' health issues (to do with physical health) and 'health in general' which referred to overall well-being (self-esteem, confidence, ability to get on with people). Both were of central concern to parents and children, and we have therefore given them more space by considering them separately. This chapter looks as physical health; the next two chapters deal with emotional and social well-being.

In the main, caring for children's physical health was discussed as an integral part of parenting. During the interviews there were lengthy descriptions of how parents cared for their children's present health. Their main concerns were clearly focused not on the treatment of particular current illnesses, but on lifestyle issues aimed at preventing future ill health. The main concerns were:

- sex
- diet

- exercise

- addictions.

Sex

Although Freud and others have portrayed the early years as having sexual aspects, conventionally sexual development has been seen as starting with puberty. However, it proved to be already a major concern for parents of this younger age group. The prospect of puberty was widely discussed in group and individual interviews:

> Well, she is developing I feel at quite a rapid pace, and I think she is about to start her menstrual cycle ... I mean it could be another year yet I suppose but I feel it's sort of on the verge just now, yes — I think there's two of them in the class that have already started their menstrual cycle and...and when I heard about these other children, it made me think.

Some parents of older children seemed acutely aware of them as imminently sexually active, and they were anxious to prepare them adequately for this.

Parental concerns were most acute in relation to girls. Boys' needs in relation to sexual development were discussed in much less detail, perhaps partly because the onset of puberty is on average later in boys, perhaps also because the majority of our respondents (and interviewers) were primarily female. There was only discussion of 'wet dreams' in two all-female gatherings and the subject was raised somewhat nervously and with a degree of embarrassed humour.

In terms of parental worries about their children's sexual behaviour, by far the main fear was that they would become infected with Aids through unprotected sex. Perhaps surprisingly, teenage pregnancy was mentioned less often and only one mother expressed a specific concern that her son would become involved in a sexual relationship too early. Two parents spoke of how difficult it would be to know how to respond to a son who was homosexual.

Although there was unanimous agreement that children should be well prepared for puberty, many parents found it difficult to give information to their children about sexuality and associated bodily changes. The sensitivity of this topic has been widely acknowledged (Sex Education Forum 1994). Even parents with a professional background in this could find it difficult:

> Although I talk to a lot of other kids about sexuality, teenagers, sex and stuff, when it comes to your own, there is this sort of, oh it's a bit daunting.

The difficulty was compounded when parent and child were of a different sex as this single mother explained:

> I mean I've got three sons and I find it hard to try and explain something to [them] ... if there's a guy there, great, you can pass it over but I think most women in the past say oh well it's his daddy that'll speak to him about his wet dreams and this and that.

In fact there were several examples given of children initiating discussion of sex with a parent of the opposite gender which may indicate that children found this less embarrassing than parents:

> So I was making the breakfast and she said 'Dad, Dad, what's an orgasm?'. [I said] 'We'll talk about it later'. You know, completely off guard at eight o'clock in the morning... I need time to think about this and how to approach it.

Although discussing sex was difficult, there was virtually unanimous agreement that parents should play their part in sex education. It was quite common for parents to buy children 'About my Body' books, some reading them through with their children and others responding to questions as they came up. Some rural parents found that car journeys to and from leisure activities could provide an opportunity for discussion of subjects such as teenage pregnancy whilst television documentaries and soaps could also help to trigger discussion of sensitive topics.

In summary, sex was viewed as a major concern by parents, and sex education was seen as a subject which should be handled with skill and with which parents needed support. In marked contrast, the children we met seemed largely oblivious of these issues. The topics of puberty, menstruation, sex, pregnancy and Aids were hardly mentioned by individuals, and were only raised in one group. This was a group of primary 7s in a rural school, and there was evidence that their awareness of these issues may have been heightened by a recent focus on them by their teacher, but even they only referred to them briefly. This lack could of course have been due to embarrassment about discussing them with outsiders, but it could equally well have been due to their being future concerns which were not salient to children in the context of their present lives.

Indeed, contrary to their parents' views, most of the children appeared to have retained a remarkably romantic innocence. Where children did talk of 'girlfriends' and 'boyfriends' the concerns were emotional rather than sexual; the stuff of Mills and Boon rather than Jackie Collins:

> I've been heartbroken lots of times. [What sort of things?] Well, my boyfriend, right, he was going out with me, right...and then he was going out with somebody else, and he never told me, and then the girl he was going out with told me — He kids on he goes out with you.

'Going out with' for this age group currently denotes simply that a boy and a girl have, so to speak 'plighted their troth'. It does not, as countless children have impatiently pointed out to their parents mean that they actually *go* anywhere together. It is therefore a highly romantic notion in itself.

Diet

Recent health promotion schemes have focused heavily on the importance for health of a diet high in fruit, vegetables and fibre and low in fat and sugar. The message seems to have got home in what families say even if not in what they do. Parents and children in all three geographical areas took it as self-evident that fruit and vegetables promoted health and that fatty foods, sweets and sugary drinks were bad for you. Good diet was generally seen by parents as essential for health and there were widespread concerns that children preferred sweets, sugary drinks and fatty foods to fruit and vegetables.

Nutritional advice easily becomes bound up with morals as 'healthy' becomes identified with 'good' and 'unhealthy' with 'reprehensible' (Backett 1992). For both parents and children, eating fruit and vegetables and avoiding sweets were seen not only as healthy but as a sign of competence, almost of good character. Giving an example in another context of his son's good sense, a father explained:

> Like he doesn't like runner beans, he doesn't like vegetables, but he eats it, but he knows it's for a reason, it's for his health. He doesn't eat it because I'm forcing it down his throat 'cause I'm certainly not. But he'll eat veg because he knows it's good for him.

Similarly children, while frankly admitting to enjoying and eating sweets, saw this nonetheless as a character defect. For example in one group, they agreed that a boy's mother was a particularly good parent because she only let her son have a small amount of chocolate for his play piece, in contrast with the giant bars they regularly consumed. They were critical of another child in the group who was allowed an unlimited supply of sweets, seeing him as 'spoiled'.

Though undoubtedly seen as important, diet was nevertheless only one consideration and factors other than health influenced what children ate. Parents aimed for a 'good enough' rather than a perfect diet, allowing their children to eat unhealthy food as long as it was not the only component. This mother's comment was typical:

> I think healthy food is what they do eat most of the time. We do have a lot of junk stuff as well but basically we do have the meat and the vegetables ... They eat an awful lot of fruit. They must be healthy children eating so much fruit.

Likewise, other parents tolerated the fact that their children ate 'pot noodles and a roll and crisps' at lunchtime because they knew they would have a 'good' meal in the evening.

The idea that a certain amount of poor quality food was difficult to avoid and could be tolerated was expressed quite often. This was partly because other aspects of their lives were seen as equally important, such as allowing children choice in what they ate or joining friends in a social event which involved eating 'junk food', or not offending grandparents who offered food that was not necessarily desirable. Parents took a pragmatic stance, which recognised that food in our culture, as in others, has a social as well as a nutritional function, and that children's rights to good health were often in tension with their right to choose.

This was very clearly brought out in our conversations with children in both studies. Food was seen by them as necessary to survival, but also as carrying a symbolic meaning. In the prompt card exercise, some children in the Parenting study thought the card saying '[parents should] feed you and care for you' was basically the same as the one that said '[parents should] love you'. Food was seen as a token of affection in both studies, particularly by younger children. One eight-year-old said he knew his mother loved him when she gave him a piece of chocolate cake, but 'healthy' foods such as soup, milk and fruit were also quoted as signs of love.

As in other areas of their lives, children did not simply take what they were given, but influenced what was offered. Some mothers accepted their children's decision, for example to become vegetarian, and tried to ensure that their overall diet took account of this. One mother explained how she responded to her children's preference for 'quick' meals:

> 'Cause I find they're in to a lot of these quick meal things. When it comes to meat they've no time for it, 'cause like I used to make steak pie and it's you know they're eating the pastry and leaving the meat. So it's like quick things they're looking for so they can go out.

Thus children's preferences did to some extent influence what they ate at home, though it was also common for parents to indicate that they controlled what was provided because, if given the choice, children would eat 'rubbish':

> I mean given the choice my boys would have, well one would have beefburger, chips and beans every night and the other would have sausage, beans and chips every night, but they don't get that every night.

Lack of money affected what food parents were able to offer their children. One single father had to consider how much electricity would be needed to cook certain dishes and another relied on visits to his parents for the children to get treats such as fresh orange juice and ice cream. A group of single mothers discussed how having a low income affected what you could buy and consequently the messages about healthy eating conveyed to children:

> You can go and get about four white loaves, the cheap loaves, compared to one brown loaf, so if you've got limited finances you go for the four, know what I mean — But then I'm not really encouraging my kids to be very healthy by saying you pile in the white loaves because it's cheaper —... But then I'm not really showing my kids the right way either, doing it that way, because they're seeing me buy the cheaper things to feed them basically rather than going and getting the brown loaf.

Likewise a group of fathers living in a low-income neighbourhood spoke of the need to shop around for the cheapest food, which they acknowledged was often not healthy.

Parents were also sometimes sceptical of some of the messages about healthy eating that children absorbed at school:

> M. will come in after they've had their health talk at school...and say 'I want to eat less meat and more vegetables'. I try to explain to him but most of your meal contains mostly vegetables you know what I mean, he has like tatties, peas and carrots sort of thing, a quarter of what you're eating is only meat the rest is all veg ... most people's diet is the vast majority of it is vegetables. You don't eat the same things all the time, I mean you try and vary things but most of your diet really is in one way or another vegetables...

Similarly a father was not convinced by his son's arguments for semi-skimmed milk and less fat in the diet:

> ... they listen to health promotion things but, the way it's portrayed, things like healthy eating, children tend to pick up on one element of it, the last thing that somebody says ... my son came back [from school] and said 'I have to start taking semi skimmed milk. I shouldn't have this kind of meat. I shouldn't be having butter. I should be having whatever'. All these things are fine as long as you don't take too much of them. Anything in excess is going to cause problems. The children need full cream milk for their bodies to grow, for the calcium, and certainly the girls need more than the boys for later years and so we've had arguments about it ... It's trying to get the balance.

This notion of balance influenced parents' views on several topics and is consistent with findings from Backett's study of middle-class families' health beliefs (1992). In this way some parents sought to influence not only their child's present diet but the way in which their children would respond to health education itself. As in other areas of children's lives, parents expected to be in control and to moderate children's ideas and actions on the basis of their own superior understanding.

Parents were able to influence what their children ate in a range of ways. Since they usually decided what would be served at meal times they had a degree of control over the family diet. However children could not be forced to eat what they did not like and parents employed a range of strategies to encourage them to eat healthily:

- explaining negative consequences of poor eating
- making healthy food attractive
- encouraging an interest in preparing food
- rationing 'undesirable' food.

Many parents strongly encouraged children to eat fruit and vegetables and talked of 'drumming the message into their heads'. One mother let her daughter help her chop up vegetables then eat them with dips while another made a lot of pasta because her children were always busy and wouldn't take time to chew. A rural mother who was concerned about her son's love of fizzy drinks limited the money he had to spend at school to prevent him from buying too many from the tuck shop. Several parents rationed how many sweets children were allowed, either to certain days of the week or by only allowing children to have sweets after they had eaten their meal.

Reflecting the fact that preparing children for the future was a significant part of parenting at this stage, a number of parents said they were not only interested in what children ate now but in teaching them healthy eating patterns for the future. At the same time they believed that children's tastes would change and that they would develop more sensible eating habits as they grew up:

> You hope that as the years go on, well you hope as they go into their teens they'll learn sense — I think your tastes do change — Yes they do change — That's right. I used to not eat sprouts when I was younger but I do now.

Thus present concerns about poor diet were kept in perspective by believing that a combination of parental instruction, inculcating good habits and a natural progression towards sensible eating would lead to a healthy diet in adult life. These views to some extent replicated parents' general perceptions and hopes about bringing up children, reflecting that the significance of food extended well beyond physical health. Eating well was equated with living well.

Exercise

In common with diet, exercise was seen as a key and related component of physical health. It was also seen as important for other reasons:

- mixing with other children
- having a sense of achievement
- being in the fresh air
- developing confidence.

Just as there was virtue in eating vegetables, so there was a moral element in the view that taking exercise was a sign of a good life. Parents spoke with pride about their children's energetic activities and those who did not like exercise were described as 'lazy'. Watching TV and playing computers were the exercise equivalent of consuming sweets and fizzy drinks.

Children took exercise in different forms. While the boys typically spoke of playing football and girls about going to dancing or majorettes, karate and swimming seemed to be popular with both girls and boys. Activities like swimming and football could be enjoyed as part of a formal organisation or informally with friends or parents. Although there were fewer opportunities for rural children to join clubs, parents described them spending long hours in energetic play outside which was not mentioned in relation to children living in either area of the city. Many of the parents who did not allow their children to play outside for safety reasons spontaneously acknowledged that this reduced opportunities for exercise which might put their health at risk in the longer term.

Parents referred to a range of parental tasks and roles to encourage their children to take exercise. On a practical level, parents (usually mothers) had to make sure that any necessary kit was washed and ready. Those who had cars drove children to clubs or classes while others accompanied them on foot or public transport. Fathers often had a role in supporting their sons' interests in more male activities such as football.

It is interesting that, apart from those in the rural area, parents saw exercise almost exclusively as something special that required organisation (and often a trip in the car) to accomplish. None of the urban parents talked about their children taking exercise in the course of getting on with daily life: walking to school or to activities, helping in the garden, walking the dog. In recent years, health promotion programmes aimed at adults have emphasised the value of incorporating regular physical activity of this kind into everyday life, but it seems that parents perhaps did not recognise its worth in relation to their children.

Surprisingly, the children seemed more aware of the message. In their drawings, exercise was a regular feature distinguishing 'healthy' from 'unhealthy' people as these quotes illustrate:

[Prompt about the meaning of 'Healthy'] My sister and her friend go jogging round the tracks.

[Prompt about the meaning of 'Unhealthy'] P sits in the house all day — we go down for him, but he says he can't be bothered coming out. And when he does come out, he'll just sit there and if we play chases he doesn't try very hard … And when we play Den, he just lets us in cos he just can't be bothered putting his hand out.

As this shows, most children did not see exercise as something separate from other activities; it occurred in the course of them, a health education message they were aware of:

I saw an advert once…it shows you all walking, and then it shows you rugby and football and it says like walk a mile and it's the same as doing so much rugby and football.

Taking your dogs for a walk, cos that can help you lose weight as well … Just walk with your dogs.

It was clear that family attitudes about the benefits of exercise were crucial in shaping their children's thinking on this. They were displayed both by precept and example:

[My mum says] go out and run about and play and get it all out your system so that when you come in you'll be tired and you'll want to go to bed.

My dad loves walking… If it's a nice day he walks to work and he walks back from work … He's always saying you should always walk to school. You should always walk to work.

Granny, she takes me lots of walks. Like she lives in … and she walks into town from there and doesn't get the bus or anything.

Addictions

Many young people view drug education programmes with a degree of scepticism. They point out with some justice that the adults who warn them of the dire effects of illegal drugs are in fact users themselves of substances (such as tobacco and alcohol) that in terms of damage to health and addictive potential are at least as harmful. This gap between the perceptions of the two generations was also obvious in our studies. As far as parents were concerned, alcohol, smoking and illegal drugs were all cited as health risks but their preoccupations with them were at odds with those of the children.

Alcohol

While total abstention was aimed for with illegal drugs and smoking, all parents considered moderate use of alcohol acceptable and some expressed the view that it was helpful gradually to introduce children to social drinking, for example by giving them an alcoholic drink on special occasions. Only a few parents expressed specific concerns about alcohol abuse, though one group of fathers were dismayed about the relatively new 'alcoholic pop' and the ease with which it could be obtained and drunk.

Most children also saw moderate consumption of alcohol in a positive light (see Fossey 1994; Laybourn, Brown and Hill 1996). Many said they had tried alcoholic drinks. They knew that alcohol could make people drunk and out of control, but also that it was an enjoyable and accepted part of the ritual of social occasions, and as such was not worrying:

> My dad's friend owns a pub...and he keeps filling the glasses up, so my mum says 'Oh I've got to go, got to go' but they won't let her go, because they are having too much fun, and my dad he just forgets that they are there and they sit talking.

However, a minority of children were troubled by adults who misused alcohol, either by being harassed by them in the street, or by seeing it in the home:

> [My dad] was in the house and he lay down on the floor just behind the bed and I was worried because he just went bang into the heater next to him ... I hate it when he's drunk.

Smoking

As far as addictive substances were concerned, children undoubtedly viewed smoking as the principal health hazard. They knew that it was addictive, causes a number of types of cancer and can kill. They also knew of its association with respiratory illness and heart disease. Many said spontaneously that their parents smoked and that they wished they wouldn't. Parents confirmed that their children lectured them on the risks involved and expressed intense dislike of smoke-filled rooms.

Children showed a sophisticated understanding of the reasons why their parents smoked:

> To comfort them — my mum says it comforts her ... — Parents smoke sometimes for the stress at work and stuff like that.

One girl's account of how her mother became addicted is particularly interesting in the way it mirrors parental fears about peer pressure on children to take illegal drugs:

> My mum was a teenager – she was about 16, these girls kept forcing her to have a cigarette…and she kept saying 'No' and they kept forcing her. And then she tried it. And then she got addicted to it.

However, despite their children's fear and revulsion about smoking, many parents, particularly in the rural area and the city scheme, seemed to take it for granted that their children would at least experiment with cigarettes.

> My Dad said that everyone usually has to try it just to see what it's like.

Most parents did not like the idea of their children taking up smoking. Some blamed themselves for setting a bad example, and tried to warn against it but feared the temptation would be too strong, as it had been for them. They thus had very confused emotions about the whole issue, which could make it hard for them to deal with it rationally:

> My childminder, she smokes. She's got this boy about 13, and [one morning] he had nicotine, tobacco all over his hand, and she says 'P what have you got on your hand?' and he says 'Nothing'. And my childminder doesn't slap or anything, but she goes like that 'Don't smoke again!' and he said 'But you smoke'. This is the first time she ever slapped him I think, but [with him] answering back she slapped him up and down the hall 13 times.

Illegal drugs

In contrast to the comparative equanimity with which they regarded smoking and alcohol, parents discussed illegal drugs at considerable length and with great fear. Almost all parents were concerned about their own lack of knowledge and experience in relation to drugs and this undoubtedly added to their anxiety. They felt unable to inform or adequately prepare their children; nor were they confident that they would be able to spot if their children were using drugs. The following comments from a single father reflect the views of many:

> One thing does worry me is this drugs scene these days. Because going through adolescence or going through the rebellious, any other stage, even becoming an adult and being allowed to drink, umpteen different things like that, I can talk from a wee bit of experience, but drugs? Maybe I was totally naive but I've never come across people taking drugs or anything like that. Even when I was a student. I mean there was smoking dope and that sort of thing, and we all did have a shot of that – but nothing so serious as what's going on … and you hear of kids being

involved and parents saying, We had no idea. I worry about that because there are tell-tale signs for most things but they're talking about there's no tell-tale signs for this, and they're taking this and you may not know. I find that morbid because I don't like to get caught out. Not for my benefit, you know. I would hate to think that anyone can be involved in something like that and I just didn't know.

Parents' fears stemmed partly from their awareness that drugs would be readily available for their children. Several parents who lived in the city schemes said that nine-year-olds in their locality were using drugs and in the suburban area there were also tales of older brothers and sisters giving drugs to primary school children. The rural parents were pretty sure that their children would not be offered drugs while they were at primary school, but there had recently been drug-related arrests in a nearby town and this had shaken their complacency about living in a safer area. Clearly part of parental anxiety about drugs was the fear that one experiment could have fatal consequences. Media coverage of cases such as that of Leah Betts have undoubtedly raised awareness of this possibility. In contrast, cigarettes or alcohol, though in reality just as addictive, are seen as 'safer', at least in the short term.

In that context it was worrying that neither parents nor children made any reference to the risks of solvent abuse, which is quite common and can be lethal in its effects (Ives 1991). Recent reports have suggested that this is a major hidden addiction problem on which health education agencies should focus urgently. Our conversations with parents and children confirms this suggestion.

The unanimous opinion of parents was that children should avoid illegal drugs altogether and some advocated health education campaigns which would 'terrify' them. No parent suggested that children should be taught how to use drugs 'safely'. Parents saw drugs as a major health education issue and wanted information for themselves and their children.

In contrast, children seemed relatively untroubled by anxieties about this issue. Conversations with children in the Parenting study showed they were certainly aware of the dangers of drugs, and had absorbed health education messages about 'saying no'. However, the risks that illegal drugs presented to their own personal physical and social well-being seemed to be retained mainly as 'background information'; known theoretically, but not of immediate relevance to their own lives. What did worry some children, notably those in the city schemes and rural areas, was the fear of being harassed by other people who had taken drugs. However, again, the focus of concern was different from that of parents. Children were not primarily worried about these users persuading or coercing them to experiment themselves; as with alcohol they simply found the behaviour of people who were under the influence of these mood-altering substances alarming and upsetting:

> This man, he had this drug needle, and I was out there, we were all watching him, he was drunk as well that time, and he threw the drug needle out, and we all stepped back and we screamed, and then he went up and picked it up and picked it up again and squashed it in his arm.

The contrast between children's and parents' views on addictive substances is very striking:

- *Alcohol*: Neither group was much concerned about the risks of children drinking. Some children were concerned about the behaviour of adults when drinking

- *Illegal drugs*: Parents were very concerned about children using drugs. Children were only concerned about the behaviour of adults and other young people when using them.

- *Smoking*: Parents did not want children to take up smoking but were resigned to them at least 'experimenting'. Children were very much concerned about the risks of parents smoking.

- *Solvents*: Neither parents nor children were at all concerned about or apparently aware of the risks.

Overall, while parents were highly anxious about the possibility of their children becoming addicted to illegal drugs, they viewed the possibility of them using other addictive substances (alcohol, solvents and tobacco) with comparative complacency. Yet many more children do become addicted to smoking, glue sniffing and drinking than to illegal drugs, and they are in fact therefore more at risk from them.

We do not of course suggest that parents were wrong to be alert to the dangers of drug addiction. However, as with stranger danger, it could be that a focus on future and hypothetical risks are diverting them from their children's own immediate concerns. In particular, the complacency with which those who smoked themselves regarded their own smoking, its effect on their children's health and the prospect of their children experimenting with cigarettes contrasted with the fear and panic engendered by illegal drugs. In this they are of course reflecting our society's inconsistent attitudes. Children are past masters at spotting double standards.

Conclusion

Although this chapter and our questioning on which it was based has focused on physical health, the reader may have been struck by the near absence of any reference to children's actual illnesses or disabilities. Current ill health was not a significant concern of the parents and children we saw. Possibly our samples included few families with serious conditions. In the general population as many as one in five children have a chronic illness, whilst headaches, allergies, colds and flu are very common (Sweeting and West 1996). However, like the health promotion literature (Sharpe, Manthner and France-Dawson 1996), it seems that most parents and children see health mainly in terms of a menu of diet, sex, exercise and addictive substances likely to affect future rather than current health prospects.

As on other issues, children's and parents' views on physical health and well-being did not always coincide. Parents were extremely concerned about sex and drugs, issues which appeared to be of little immediate interest to the children who were far more worried by the risks of smoking. Food was, of course, a topic of great interest to both!

What is particularly interesting and encouraging, however, is the degree to which children were aware of and understood those current health issues that they saw as relevant to them. Whether or not they all obeyed them, they were certainly well aware of recent messages about healthy eating and about exercise as part of daily living; in some respects more so than their parents. And they showed a remarkably sophisticated understanding of the pressures that lead adults to become addicted to tobacco. All this suggests that middle childhood may be a crucial period for communicating with children about health matters. They are old enough to understand the issues; young enough to view them objectively.

In this sense parents seem to be right when they spoke of middle childhood as their 'last chance' to influence their children before the pressures of the teenage culture hit them. However perhaps parents need to rethink how they go about seizing this chance. The issue of addictions is a case in point. The children we spoke to were totally opposed to drug taking and smoking, yet we know that by the mid-teen years they will regard them differently, and that many of them will in fact go on to try both (West and Sweeting 1992). What perhaps is needed from parents is a move away from attempts simply to 'warn' and 'terrify' children against negative influences, in favour of more open and egalitarian discussion of their consequences which starts from the children's own concerns and understanding. The confidence and subtlety with which most parents handled the familiar issue of healthy eating indicates how well they can engage with their children's perspective, given the knowledge and confidence to do so.

CHAPTER 7

Well-being, Stress and Support: Inside the Family

Introduction

As we saw in the last chapter, parents saw health as including both physical and emotional well-being. They were keen to promote both. However, in practice they had much less to say on the emotional and social needs of their children than on their physical health and safety. It was not that they were unconcerned about this aspect of their children's lives; rather that in comparison with other issues their concerns about emotional well-being were in the background rather than the foreground of their thoughts. This is in line with the traditional adult perspective of mid-childhood as a comparatively carefree uncomplicated time. As we saw in earlier chapters parents did identify a number of social and personal stresses on their children, which they saw as creating anxiety for them as parents. However, their focus was largely on the outside world of strangers (peer pressure and stranger danger) or on the future (academic success and employment). In view of the tenor of previous chapters it will come as no surprise that the children identified a different set of stresses, which related to the here and now and their immediate social environment. For them, the chief source of both stress and well-being were their current relationships with:

- family members
- friends and peers.

In the present chapter we look at children's relationships within the family, including extended family. In the next chapter we consider their relationships with outsiders, in particular with other children.

Parents, while acknowledging the routine irritations of family life, seemed to see the home basically as a safe haven, a comfortable and cosy nest away from the pressures and dangers of the outside world. The picture given by children was much more mixed. They were aware of the important role of the family in promoting their emotional well-being, and of the help it could provide when things went wrong. However, they also spoke vividly of family relationships as a major source of stress.

Parents – as seen by children and by parents themselves

> If I'm going out somewhere, my mum always says I look lovely, and I really love you, and she always says that to me. ... My dad doesn't say that but ... he always makes sure I'm wrapped up warm, and if I'm out with just a T-shirt he comes out and gives me a jumper or a jacket to put on ... He tries to get home from work early or he'll take half days and work extra time at the weekends so that he'll be there for me getting home from school when my Mum's at work.

This quote from a nine-year-old girl indicates the many small details that go towards a child's sense of being loved and cared for. Many children cited their parents as important sources of support. Parents were described as boosting their children's confidence and self-esteem by showing affection, recognising achievements and praising effort. They contributed greatly to their children's enjoyment of life by sharing time and activities with them.

> [I'm happy] at all my birthdays, when my parents take me out and everything.

However, for some children parents could also be a source of distress in a number of ways. Unfair treatment was greatly resented. Although children did not normally cite parental punishment as a cause of upset, they did if there was some unfairness involved, often in relation to a sibling:

> Something that would hurt me would probably be ... if my brother annoyed me and then I tell my Mum, and then I usually sometimes get shouted at, and my Mum says you're older and should know, so that's what makes me hurt, and like I get the blame for it.

Letting children down and not keeping promises was another way in which parents upset children:

> I was going to see my dad, it was a Monday, and I had to take a day off school and then he wasn't there ... And I went all the way down to Glasgow. ... I feel sad when he doesn't come ... He keeps getting mixed up with all the days.

Children were also upset by arguments between parents, even where these might not be considered significant from the adult point of view:

> Because sometimes maybe your mum and dad or something, maybe just think it's ... having a little argument, but it isn't, it's bad, it's really sad for you and they don't understand.

Well, when we lived in London, my mum and dad started fighting, and I was about three years old when this happened, and I was trying to stop them from arguing, so I went up to my room and I started crying then.

Part of the anxiety seems to relate to fears that arguments were an omen of something worse, and certainly the high prevalence of separation and divorce has created a climate where this is a real fear for children. Actual marriage breakdowns caused complications and distress to some in the sample:

Every time we go to see my dad we can't spend any time with him, 'cause we've always got to go to M's house – that's my dad's girlfriend, and I was really looking forward to getting a day on my own with dad, and we had to go to M's again, 'cause they'd already arranged it.

A boy acted out his real life worry in a role play:

My mum and dad are splitting up, but I don't want them to, and they are fighting over who I am going to live with.

On the other hand, most children recognised that though their parents sometimes caused them pain, they were vital sources of help and comfort when other things went wrong. Parents supported their children in a number of ways. Physical comfort was welcomed by children of all ages, boys as well as girls:

When my papa died and my dad gave me a cuddle, I found that helpful.

Parents could help children in their relationships with others:

My mum, if I've had a fight with my friend, she'll help me make friends with her again.

They could also help them understand situations by sympathetic explanation or providing them with 'cover stories' to present to others:

I used to be sad [and teased] because I was dyslexic, but then my mum said, it's an advantage for other stuff like ... I'm not very good at reading and writing, so that means I'm good at art and stuff, imaginary stuff.

Some children were particularly close to their parents: e.g. 'I can tell my mum anything'. Such children appreciated parents' sensitivity to their feelings and their respect for their wishes:

Whenever I'm sat there, they always come over, my dad always says 'What's wrong?' 'cause he can always tell by my face.

This boy spoke of the thoughtful way his parents responded to his problems, usually discussing with him how he wanted them to help:

They say, well they ask me 'Do you want me to handle it?' [Bullying] I usually say I'll handle it first, and then if I can't get them to stop, I'll go and talk to them.

Many children were very appreciative of their parents' efforts to help, and said they were the first people they would turn to with a problem. However, a significant minority were quite critical of their parents' responses to them.

Part of the problem was that parents tended to 'screen out' matters which they considered unimportant such as children's 'tiffs'. Minimisation of this kind by parents (or indeed denial that there was a problem) was something that children found unhelpful. As we shall see later, they particularly complained that parents failed to realise how hurtful teasing by peers and friendship difficulties can be:

> [Parents] don't understand, they don't realise what happens to children ... They would say stuff like 'Oh, don't be silly, and go and play'.

A similar problem arose with parental attempts at reassurance. This was sometimes seen as helpful, but only in the context of first taking the child's concerns seriously. Trotting out a formula gave the impression that worries and their causes were devalued or not understood:

> [Parents] are all saying 'Don't worry' they never say anything else. They just say 'Don't worry', they never help you — It's only words. It's not feelings — it's only words — It's not helping you, it's just, like what they think, but it doesn't.

An older girl who was upset when her mother periodically left her alone in the house without telling her where she was going, contrasted the response 'Don't be silly, you're old enough now' with the real reassurance she wanted, which included physical comfort, recognition of her fears, and a promise to do something about them:

> What would you have liked her to say?] 'Okay darling', and cuddle me and that, 'See I was only going to be with R' or something and she'll tell me the next time she does it and stuff like that.

In the above examples, children had at least felt able to confide in their parents. However it was clear that this did not always happen. Deterrents to confiding included fear that a confidence would not be respected, guilt about wrongdoing, doubt about being believed, or fear of appearing foolish for not being able to cope:

> The most frightened. It was probably when I was alone in the house once, it was only for about half an hour, I guess ... [the dog] started growling as if someone was there ... [Did you tell anyone? Can I ask you why you wouldn't have said?] I

don't know why. Well, probably because once they were back I kind of felt a wee bit silly that I was frightened and I can't believe why I was.

The most common complaint children had, however, was that their parents simply didn't have time for them. Several group discussions focused partly around this theme. The chief reason for the problem was that parents were too busy and preoccupied:

> I asked my mum to play with me and she said no, she was too busy doing the washing — My mum said she would play Monopoly with me three days ago, she hasn't because she's doing so much stuff for my sister — I don't ask my mum to do anything, cos she's got the baby to feed — my mum and dad are too busy.

Part of the difficulty seemed to be that parents were working during the day, and needed the evenings and weekends to catch up on other chores. This could lead to them not noticing how a child was feeling, or not listening to them properly:

> Like sometimes I have problems, and my mum and dad can't see it, because they're like, well, my dad's cooking, and my mum's probably like, cleaning up the place.

> Cos they're so busy they don't notice — When you're sitting down and you want your mum and dad to talk to you and they're too busy.

This was given as one of the reasons why a child might be 'sad or worried most of the time':

> If her mum is always away at work and her dad's out — she's not happy.

When a parent has too much to do it can also lead to the false reassurance referred to earlier — it is quicker to make an instant standard response such as an offhand 'don't worry' rather than take the time to hear the child out and put affection and feeling into the reply. 'It's only words', as one child said. However, some of this group did feel their parents could give a more genuine response and still care even though at work:

> Some people do — People that have got more time to spend with their children can — But I would say that the people who are working are usually thinking about their children, although they don't say it … — Yes definitely — My mum listens to me.

While many children in the groups were openly critical of their parents' inattention to them, other children interviewed individually were more accepting, and saw it as their responsibility to judge the moment for a confidence:

> My mum, like if she's busy, then I don't tell her, 'cause then she would just say 'not now, tell me later' but she does listen to me.

However, there is something rather bleak in their very acceptance that adults will not notice hurts and anxieties because of other preoccupations:

> 'Cause they've got to worry about money, the bank, eh paying the bills and things, and sometimes they can't handle children when they're about their feet sometimes. Like if they've got really, really important things. I don't blame them much. [Do you think grown ups ever just don't care how children are feeling?] No, I think they care a lot, they just don't have the time.

On this issue the children's views were mirrored by those of parents. Parents were aware of the importance of spending time and listening, but acknowledged that this was not necessarily easy to put into practice. Those who had several children or whose work was demanding admitted they did not always have enough time or energy to respond sensitively to problems. Similarly parents who were under financial or other pressures could be too preoccupied to respond appropriately when a child sought attention. While recognising that the ever-attentive parent was an unrealistic ideal, mothers and fathers still expressed considerable guilt that they were not as available for their children as they thought they should be, as this father of four explains:

> I think it would be nice to be able to spend more time with them. It would be nice to be able to be more relaxed and not be angry at times and so on. The simple fact is there are so many pressures on and you hear all the other parents saying all the same things as we're saying, if only we were better, if only we were nicer people and so on. We're not ogres, the children are happy children but at times you just wish you would just relax a bit more and give them more time.

In addition to having enough time and energy, other factors influenced parents' ability to provide support through listening. Where discussion was not part of the family culture it was difficult for parents to introduce it at this stage. A group of mothers in the city scheme described how they tried to get their children to talk to them but their efforts usually ended in the parents losing their tempers in frustration.

Children's behaviour was a factor in itself. Parents from all areas described individual children who were uncommunicative, in which case parents had to watch for signs of distress and encourage them to talk. For example, one father found out that his son's sore stomachs were a sign of his unhappiness at school. Effective listening could be difficult if children talked too much, as well as very little. When children were very voluble, parents could not respond to everything and had to try to work out what was important and needed more attention. Naturally this was based on parents' own priorities so that, for example, (as the children pointed out) friendship disputes were filtered out as relatively trifling matters whereas anything to do with sex, drugs or bullying was considered important, and attention paid to it.

Although most children saw the main barrier to communication as lying with the adults, some admitted they did not always want to talk to their parents about sensitive matters. There was, for example, reluctance among some older children to involve adults in peer disputes. They pointed to the imbalance of power which can make it harder to sort things out if parents become involved. For instance, parents may tell you not to be friends with the person again, but that contradicts a child's notion of what friendship is about. In these cases, as we will see later, other children may make better confidants.

Sisters and brothers

The happiest [I've ever been] em was when ... K was born, even though it was four o'clock in the morning ... my friend Christopher was staying the night, and he wanted to name her! ... I was actually thinking that it may be a few more weeks or months, because it was quite a surprise!

When your wee sister hits you, you're angry that she hits you, but you're happy because you know she'll get into trouble.

As these two accounts show, sibling relationships normally evoke a mixture of emotions and vary from the very close and positive to the extremely negative (see Kosonen 1996). They were a source of great pleasure and support to some children and a constant irritation to others. Complaints about siblings included messing up your room; fighting; getting you into trouble, and getting preferential treatment from parents. On the other hand, they could be a real help, especially during disputes:

Well, my brother would stick up for me — I would stick up for my wee sister.

For some children they were also an important source of emotional support, offering help and advice where parents had failed:

I tell my sister sometimes ... She talks to me if I get angry, she just says things like 'Calm down' and she puts her arm round me and she says it's okay, because that happens to other people every day.

Other children also described the feeling of solidarity that comes from facing a joint problem:

When my mum and dad are arguing, me and B and M just sit down and watch the TV and just worry and talk and that.

> When I get a row or something K [18-year-old sister] always helps me ... She just says, it's okay, I'm always getting a row too, and things like that.

However, siblings are not universally seen as helpful in a crisis:

> [When you're feeling worried do you tell anybody?] Yes, usually my brother. [What does he say?] He just says don't be such a wimp, or something like that. [Is that a help?] No.

Other relatives

Although they were not often mentioned, it was clear that for some children the extended family was an important adjunct to emotional well-being.

> When my relations come up I feel really, really happy.

For most children, their grandparents seemed of greatest significance, though a few, mainly from ethnic minority families, also mentioned cousins and aunts. It was pointed out to us that grandparents usually have more time, and may become alternative, more accessible and comforting sources of support when parents are busy:

> My gran understands more, I think — I speak to her, she's got more time, my mum's at work and that — I go to my grandpa's on Wednesdays, and he's 74, and he's got more time to talk to me and help me with my homework and that. ... — Grandparents are not working so they have got a lot of time to talk to you.

In contrast with parents and siblings, grandparents were described in a wholly positive light by the children who mentioned them. They were only a source of unhappiness in death. This was an event which many children had experienced and it constituted one of the most frequently mentioned causes of sadness:

> When my grandad died ... that was the saddest I've ever felt and everybody was sad at that point, and that was really sad, and then my great grandma heard the news and a couple of days after she died as well.

Pets

Pets were clearly identified by children as family members, and as such played an important part in their emotional lives. They were often included by children on their ecomaps as 'people who are important to me', and figured significantly in their conversations and drawings.

> Happiest ... you know, I think it's probably when I got my dog ... We got him from a home, he wasn't even a month old.

Pets were sometimes also cited as a source of comfort and support. Some children said that when upset they would talk to animals:

> If I'm upset or anything, and no one's in the house, like if my mum's away out, and my big sister's watching TV, you know, I normally take the cat and cuddle it.

As the children themselves explained, pets are in many ways the perfect confidants, offering acceptance, physical comfort, complete confidentiality and unconditional positive regard, as this group pointed out:

> It's not stupid, because it's as if they understand us — Because they can't talk back at you — Because like they cuddle into you — They won't go and tell everybody what you've been telling them — ... and they don't laugh at you and stuff — ... They're too stupid not to like you, they always like you.

Conclusion

The family (in its broadest sense) is seen by children as crucial to their emotional well-being, both in ensuring a basic level of love, security and enjoyment, and in providing help and support when things go wrong. Yet it is not an entirely comfortable place to be. Parents are clearly a valued source of support, and often the prime confidants for their children. But unfairness, preoccupation with work and finances, and parental quarrelling also upset and worry children. Parents' efforts to comfort and help their children can be blocked by a number of factors:

- lack of time to listen, understand and respond caringly
- failure to appreciate the salience of the problem to the child
- 'filtering out' of problems deemed to be unimportant.

Siblings seem to be a mixed blessing at this age; sometimes supportive, sometimes upsetting; often both by turns. Grandparents and pets, in contrast, were seen wholly positively. In their different ways they are perhaps underrated sources of support for children. Freed from the need to censure or compete, they can provide affection, acceptance and time in abundance. Neither were given much prominence by parents in their discussions, and it may be that their importance for children's emotional well-being is underestimated.

Overall, there is quite a contrast in perceptions here. Parents seemed to feel they carried all (or almost all) of the responsibility for their children's happiness, whereas children themselves appear to see themselves as drawing on a much wider pool of support. This contrast between the two views becomes even sharper as we move on to consider children's relationships with the outside world.

CHAPTER 8

Well-being, Stress and Support: Outside the Family

Introduction

We have already seen that many parents were highly anxious about specific threats to their children's physical safety outside the home. In relation to children's emotional well-being parents had an additional and more pervasive fear: that of contamination. The outside world was seen not only as dangerous but as corrupting. Some of these anxieties have already been referred to: that children would be introduced to crime or drugs through their association with other people. A further anxiety was that of peer pressure. Although known friends were valued, peers were commonly regarded as a negative influence, more likely to lead children astray than keep them on the straight and narrow. There was a strong sense of helplessness in the interviews; many parents saw their children as beleaguered by an array of potentially negative influences, which they felt powerless to counteract.

In contrast to parental pessimism, most of the children we interviewed exuded optimistic confidence about the outside world. They had a background consciousness of the risks which they could detail when asked, and some had, as we have seen, had their sense of security dented by encounters with anti-social and unpleasant individuals. However, the majority of children showed considerable confidence that adults in general were well disposed to them, and inclined to help rather than harass. And, as we shall see, they saw relationships with peers in a much more positive light than their parents did.

The children's perspective

Friends

> When [my best friend] was on holiday once ... for around 30 days ... and then another 30 days ... 'cause it was over school days she was away too, and then she came back it was probably the happiest I've ever been, because when I saw her and it was like tears came to my eyes, because it was happy tears.

One of the clearest messages that came out of our conversations with children was the important part friendships played in their lives. As the above quotation shows, close personal friendships were seen by children as central to emotional well-being. After immediate family members, friends also tended to figure highly in children's lists of the most important people in their lives or as people to turn to when in difficulty.

As other studies have shown (Hartup 1996) for girls the normal pattern was membership of a small group of close friends, and within that considerable emotional investment in one particular 'best friend'. For boys friendships were equally important, but apparently at a less intense level, with more emphasis on shared activities and identification with the group:

> [Happiness is] Being with your friends — When you score a goal — When your team wins the cup.

Involvement in friendships which are going well seems to be crucial to children's sense of emotional well-being and self-confidence. Hence, when they went wrong, they were a source of pain. Here there were gender differences too, with boys' less intense, more interest-focused friendships causing fewer, but more overt and physical, upsets, and girls' intense personal attachments causing serious trauma when they went wrong. The discussion in this mixed group illustrates the difference:

> I think girls fight more. [Do you?] Yes we do, we do. ... [Do the boys agree with that?] Well, I've never seen a fight with boys that much. When you see them, it's usually about football. I've never seen anything else ... I've never seen any other fights. [So what do girls fight about more often?] Well, sometimes you fight over your different friends. 'Cause there's one person goes away with the other friend and the other one might feel a bit upset.

The main speaker on the topic in this group continued:

> Me and R, we've got another two friends K and S, and they're best friends, and me and R are best friends and I get upset when R goes off with other friends ... and K, I don't know why she does it ... but sometimes she tries to drive you away from your other friend. ... And ... K and R said [to one another] 'Can you be my best friend?' So they came and told me and I was very upset, and I said 'R, why

can't me and you just be friends like we always did? And she said 'well, we can always play together every day, but she's my best friend now' and I was dead upset.

After this saga of betrayal had gone on for several minutes, a boy in the group commented:

> Em, when it's the girls that are fighting, their fighting is arguments, but when the boys are fighting, we're always like kicking people everywhere and that and punching and everything, aren't we, P?

The pain of losing or being let down by a friend of the same sex was frequently cited as major source of sadness and anger by girls, though it was also cited by one boy:

> The angriest I've ever felt ... One of my friends ... was going to come round to my house for me and then, we were going to play in the park and then go back to his house, and he never came.

Losing a friend meant more to children than loss of company and feelings of jealousy and rejection. It also removed from them one of their main sources of support. As we saw in the last chapter, parents are often their children's primary confidants. However, a marked finding of the Well-being study was the extent to which children also relied on each other for help and comfort.

Friends have a number of advantages over parents as confidants. First, particularly in the case of peer disputes, they have a more immediate and intuitive understanding of what the experience is like. A number of children felt that adults were too far distanced from the pain of childhood to understand what children are going through, and that in consequence their parents tended to minimise difficulties with peers as playground 'tiffs' with a simple solution for example, finding another friend to play with.

For that reason friends could sometimes be more helpful; they understand the full awfulness of the situation, and can therefore allow expression of feeling in a way that parents may not. This girl turned to another friend rather than her mother when her best friend had deserted her:

> I got really angry and we went to F's house, and we couldn't stop talking about it after that and I was really angry. [Did that help?] Uhuh.

Friends can also have a more subtle view of the problem and the very complex issues preventing its resolution. Difficulties with peer relationships and friendships are delicate situations involving many complex unwritten 'rules'. For example, girls commonly regard 'best friendships' as sacrosanct in the way that (theoretically) adults regard marriages, and it is therefore not always possible to do as parents suggest and 'find a new one' if everyone else is already paired off. In such cases friends may understand the issues better than adults:

> We can go and talk to them [friends in difficulties]— Talk them out of it — Start bossing them about like 'you should go and tell that person' — Go and apologise to them.

Again, it may be easier for children to do this than parents:

> They can talk to them, but they don't have to be on either side.

Second, friends can act as independent confidants in matters that children feel unable to discuss with parents. Many spoke of confiding in friends, secure in the knowledge that their confidences would be kept and not passed on to others. For older children this was of paramount importance. For them privacy and 'swearing to secrecy' were often essential precursors to disclosure, as is illustrated by this group role play:

> Why are you crying? — Wait till we walk up here, and I'll tell you in just a minute ... my mum's got problems, you won't tell anyone, will you? — No — Swear — I swear — Guides' honour — Guides' honour — I think my mum and dad are going to split up. They're like fighting and that, and I get upset about my dad hitting my mum, my dad gets drunk and that.

The receiving and respecting of confidences under all circumstances was seen as one of the main helping processes and a sign of true friendship:

> My friend ... she really comforts me [Does she? How?] Well, when I go to play with her, if I tell her, like a secret or something, I know that she'll keep it. ... [Even if] she says 'tell your mum', right, and if she knows I won't, she goes 'Well, I think you'd better', and things like that, but she never tells my mum, because she knows that if she tells her I won't be very happy.

Third, because they are on the same wavelength, friends can empathise and respond sensitively to a child's wishes, for example offering tacit support rather than explicit sympathy. Some children recognised that in certain circumstances, they didn't want any active help; a caring silence on the subject might be what is needed. A boy whose grandfather had just died explained:

> The day of the funeral, my friends didn't annoy me or anything like that ... K [best friend] was being very special ... just sort of being nice to me ... I didn't want to speak, keep thinking about it.

Tormentors

Whilst friendship difficulties were often acknowledged by children as something they had experienced themselves, they also referred to other peer interaction problems, sometimes affecting others more than themselves. Teasing and name-calling were frequently mentioned, and mostly encountered at school. Children are quick to pick on anyone who deviates from the group. There were many references to the way in which children who are 'different' in some way are made to feel unhappy or angry as a result of name calling or derogatory comments. There are a wide range of other characteristics which can evoke this. Amongst those mentioned were:

- wearing glasses
- freckles
- obesity
- dyslexia
- ethnicity
- clothes.

> Some girls are really terrible and everything – they always hang about with boys and everything, and they don't wear school uniform, they wear other clothes, brand names and things. And like when one of my friends were not – maybe it's trainers that's not a brand make, you know, they get teased and everything. And they tend to tease you and say 'you're so immature, you're babies and things'. And when me and my friends have fun, you know, [playing tig] they kind of comment and stuff and go 'that's so babyish' you know, and go 'Oh look at your trainers' and everything.

Verbal harassment was much more commonly reported than physical bullying, though the one could shade into the other:

> When I moved to this school, there was girls bullying me because I didn't have a school uniform yet — They were making fun of her — ... I was feeling awful upset ... — They had her up against a wall — they were pulling her clothes and that — 'Why have you not got a school uniform?'

Physical bullying at school is a problem that most children were aware of as part of their peer culture, but it was rarely reported in our sample. Stories recurred about children being picked on, hit and kicked, but mainly outside school, and mostly in relation to other people. However, a few had experienced in-school bullying themselves:

> I get bullied by D's big sisters, she's got pure big sisters. I didn't know what to do ... All D's big sisters were chasing me round twice and scaring me. I felt that scared.

Teasing and bullying occurred among both boys and girls. There were, however, slight apparent gender differences in how they viewed them. Girls spoke with more feeling about being teased and bullied, admitting to unhappiness and anxiety about both. Boys in all-boy groups frequently alluded to physical bullying, but usually talked about it in terms of fights between equals which were seen as part of everyday life:

> There's this boy called R ... in this school and ... [he] goes like that, punches me in the face, and I got a big black eye there. It's gone ... [We] sort it out ourselves.

However, this confidence may be more apparent than real; adopted as part of the macho image that fights can be taken in one's stride. In individual interviews several boys did speak with feeling about their experience of being bullied and the distress it caused them.

Again, our individual and group discussions showed clearly that many children demonstrated a responsibility to try to help others. Instances of teasing, particularly in relation to ethnic differences, were roundly condemned. In relation to bullying, more confident children sometimes had a strong identification with the underdog, and intervened individually, or united to protect a weaker child from persecution:

> There was this boy in our school, he went about picking fights with people he knew he could beat ... He started fighting with someone, and I stepped in.

> Most people in our class care about G because em I think he's got a slight problem, and T always bullies him ... If he was crying they would say, are you all right, and stuff. Come away with me and keep away from T.

Teachers

We have seen that children were strongly disposed to help each other, and provided the major source of support for each other outside the family. Nonetheless, they recognised that adults outside the family were also important for their emotional well-being.

The most significant of these were undoubtedly teachers. They were often referred to as sources of support. Children were, for example, very conscious of teachers as enhancing their self-esteem:

> Miss P, she gives you support, and she makes you feel you've done really well ... 'Cause when I wrote a story out, she said 'I can't believe how excellent that is', and she says things like that.

Children were articulate about differences among teachers and a few individuals were mentioned who were not much liked. However, the majority of children seemed to hold teachers in high regard as arbiters and sources of protection and support. One group agreed that most understand children well:

Teachers have to, because they are working with children all the time.

Nonetheless, children were well aware of the difficulty of the teacher's task in dealing with issues such as bullying. This could affect their willingness to ask for help. One important deterrent to confiding was the fear that 'telling' would only exacerbate and escalate the problem. This, of course, is a common worry in situations of bullying, and one that is difficult to reassure children on:

Well ... say if you told an adult, they might bully you even more because you told an adult. [And do you think they would be able to sort it out, would they be able to help you with that ?] Well, em no, not really.

Readiness to seek help appeared partly to depend on the child's perception of the balance of risk and pay-off in confiding. If the child is secure in the knowledge that effective action will be taken, they are more ready to confide. If action is likely to be ineffective, it is not worth it:

When I've had a fight at school, or if I've been bullied or anything, a which I hardly ever am, I just feel safe when I tell ... the teacher I'm with at the moment. She's very strict ... she'll ask for the person and give them a big row ... [but] there are some teachers I don't feel really safe with. My teacher I had last year, she was, like, she was a nice teacher, but she was too soft ... you know, the most she'll do is like, go 'Don't do it again'.

Other professionals

Class teachers were undoubtedly children's main adult source of help. However, for particular situations, other adults were mentioned who children do not normally see regularly. Social workers, 'counsellors' and guidance teachers were mentioned. Such people were respected for their special skills and knowledge of how to help young people and of the value of an objective opinion. Older children also often cited ChildLine, whose publicity is obviously successful:

They would understand you more — 'Cause they do it every day — ... Talk to complete strangers so they don't know what's been going on and they won't tell anyone ... ChildLine people are still professional. They've been to training to talk to you and stuff — ... If someone is bullying you or something, [your mum and dad] just say 'just ignore them' or something like that, but if you go to somebody professional, they can maybe do something about it.

On the other hand, a few children expressed a strong sense of family loyalty and a wish to protect their parents from outside agencies. One group of older girls from a city scheme unanimously and strongly believed that it would be wrong to talk to anyone outwith the family about problems since this might lead to social work involvement which would only add to their parents' worries:

> Your mum and dad would be, like, shocked as well — They'd go mental! They'd go mental at you. For getting the social up — ... And they'd be hurt. With the social workers asking all these questions and that — I know, they could get into major trouble.

The parents' perspective

Once again, parental perceptions of life outside the family was at marked variance with that of children. In terms of basic love and support parents saw this as emanating almost entirely from the family, and as primarily their responsibility. Teachers were occasionally mentioned as potential confidants, and one mother made a point of informing the school when there were serious family problems, encouraging her daughter to discuss personal concerns with her class teacher. This degree of openness was unusual, however. Not all parents recognised that their child might have a need for independent support, and even when they did, it was seen as coming entirely from adults.

Parents did not talk at any length (if at all) about the importance of their children's close friendships, nor did they mention them as contributing to their emotional well-being. Nor did they talk in depth about the distress caused to children when these friendships go wrong. The only references to this situation was in terms of the need to 'screen out' unimportant talk from the child about playground 'tiffs'. Parents seemed astonishingly oblivious of both the pleasure and the pain their children experienced in relation to this important aspect of their lives. Similarly, they seemed largely unaware of the myriad ways that children described of helping each other.

Where parents did talk about relationships between children it was in terms of 'peer groups' rather than friendships. As such they were seen in generalised and simplistic terms as a negative force for children's well-being. Parents' concerns were primarily focused on two major issues: bullying, and the need to win popularity by conforming to peer pressure from the group.

Bullying

On the issue of bullying (in the form of physical intimidation or assault), parents were certainly in tune with children's expressed needs. The children's accounts confirm that this is a serious problem about which they wanted something done by adults. However, parents talked very little about the much more common problem of verbal teasing, and they may underestimate the pain children also suffer as a result of this. The sheer nastiness of some of the verbal abuse children hurled at each other would have some adults phoning their lawyers if it occurred in the workplace, yet the child is often told to 'sort it out yourself'. Of course, not all children are deeply wounded by such behaviour, and some of the children, particularly boys, seemed also to feel that disputes were part of life, needing no intervention, and that they were best left to deal with things themselves. However, other children are hurt by it, and it seems a cruel irony that some of the worst behaviour from others we ever routinely have to face takes place at the point in our lives when we are least equipped to deal with it.

Peer pressure

On the issue of peer popularity, it seems that parents may well be interpreting the situation as much simpler than it is. Parents certainly placed a high value on acceptance by peers, and it was recognised that this contributed to emotional well-being. However, their efforts to facilitate it seemed to concentrate on helping their children 'fit in' with the larger group by enabling them to keep up with other children in terms of dress and lifestyle. Several discussions centred around the need to provide the 'right' trainers, with some parents on low incomes appearing to make considerable efforts to do so.

These single parents felt that their children already had so much stacked against them that they needed every help to blend in and be accepted:

> Because other kids can be very cruel as well to yours you know because your kids got no dad. Everybody's kids have got peer pressure, but it's this hassle they get from other kids, they don't want to hang about with them cos they're no wearing the right jacket or they've no got the right schoolbag, what I think are silly wee things, but to a kid that's important.

Many parents clearly felt that the issue was extremely salient to their children. Curiously, however, it appeared to be of little concern to the sample children in either study. Very few made any reference to peer pressure or to the possession of the 'right' clothes or footwear as a source of either pleasure or pain, and when they did it was as often about uniform as about leisure wear. In the Well-being study it did not emerge as a major theme in any discussion of fears and anxieties, nor did it feature in any list of things adults could do to make children happier. In fact, children in the Parenting study consistently rated buying children things as the one really unimportant aspect of parenting. When the issue of clothes was mentioned, as we have seen, it was always in the context of more general discussions of teasing and bullying, cited only as one of many other differences that might be picked on, and no more hurtful than any other.

This is perhaps surprising. Other studies have found that children are acutely aware of the need to 'fit in' and that they construct themselves in relation to their peers in a large part by consumer goods such as clothes (Miles 1996; Willis 1990). It appears that the pressure to appear fashionable increases markedly in secondary school (Middleton, Ashworth and Walker 1994), and it may be that our children were just too young to have felt their full impact. It is also possible that they did not hanker after these items because they already had them and simply took them for granted! On the other hand it is possible that while these pressures do exist (and hence are revealed when researchers focus on them specifically) they are not of major significance to children compared with other issues and hence do not make much of a showing in studies that ask them consider their lives as a whole.

In fact, children seemed much less concerned about the need to fit in with the larger group than they were with the need to maintain particular friendships within it. And where friendship difficulties arose, these were based on shifting relationships rather than on absence of material possessions.

It is interesting that parents seemed more concerned than children about this issue. One wonders whether they may be projecting some of their own feelings about status on to their children. One group of suburban parents talked about pressure from their own adult peers to keep up the affluent lifestyle, the holiday abroad, the new car. Perhaps keeping up with the Jones' children is an aspect of this. Parents were also aware of the extent to which children's material expectations are fed by advertising and the media. Perhaps their own are too.

However, another facet of the situation may be that it is simpler to verbalise and focus on the relatively simple issue of children's lifestyles rather than get drawn in to the messy and painful business of their relationships. Children seem to have good grounds for supposing that their parents do not understand the importance and complexity of their friendships. This seemed particularly to apply to problems between girls, and it may be that parents genuinely do not appreciate the depth of feeling girls of this age have for their special friends. The joy, sorrow, jealousy and anger described by some children showed an intensity much more akin to that of an adult partnership than to adult friendship. Little wonder parents were seen as missing the point when they dismissed the situation as 'just a tiff'.

Conclusion

There is no doubt of the central contribution that children make to each other's emotional well-being. They rely on their close friendships not only for a basic sense of confidence, belonging and enjoyment, but also for help and comfort in times of stress. When these relationships are disrupted they cause very troubled emotions. Parents appear to underestimate the importance of friendships for children, and the gap that is created in their lives when they go wrong.

Parents appeared to see the responsibility for their children's emotional well-being as lying almost entirely within the family (and primarily with them); in contrast children see themselves as often drawing also on outside relationships. Certainly a few parents realised that children might want to turn to outsiders for help, but they saw this almost exclusively in terms of other adults (primarily teachers). They seemed oblivious to the rich source of support most children provide for each other through close mutual friendships. Parents tended to regard peer relationships in generalised terms and largely in a negative light, as potentially corrupting rather than life enhancing.

This is worrying, not only because it may hamper a child's access to peer support, but because it indicates that parents may be oversimplifying, superimposing their fears and anxieties on to the child's situation, and failing as a result to listen to their most acute felt needs.

When children in the Well-being study were asked at the end of the interviews to brainstorm ideas for what adults could do to make children happier, the older ones came up with a clear set of priorities. The first was that adults should listen to children, attend seriously to their concerns, attempt to empathise with them and provide genuine reassurance. The second was that they should spend more time with them, to enable these things to take place. Our comparison of parental and child views confirms that these are indeed important issues for parents to consider.

CHAPTER 9

Children's Rights

Introduction

During the last decade there has been increasing attention in academic and professional circles to the notion of children's rights and in 1991 the British government ratified the UN Convention on the Rights of the Child (Asquith and Hill 1994; Franklin 1995). The rights set out in this convention can be broadly grouped into three categories:

- **P**rotection: the right to be safe.
- **P**rovision: the right to have needs met, e.g. for food, shelter and education.
- **P**articipation: the right to be consulted, depending on age and level of understanding, on any decisions which affects the child.

The principles of the Convention now form the basis of much British child care and family law. However children's rights have mainly been regarded as important for certain groups of children, notably children in public care and in specific situations, for example over consent to medical treatment or children's place of residence. Mainstream schools and parents have in many ways been left out. Outside professional and political circles, people have learned about the changes primarily through the media.

The Children Act 1989 which came into force in England and Wales in 1991 was hailed as a 'children's charter' by both advocates and critics. Subsequent publicity has fuelled this perception. There have been publicised examples of so called 'child divorce' cases when children have applied for a court order to allow them to live apart from their parents. The Children (Scotland) Act 1995 which has similar provision came into force in April 1997, albeit with much less publicity or public debate about its implications. It is noteworthy that education legislation has not incorporated similar rights for children at school but has emphasised parental rights (Sinclair 1996).

The other main issue which has brought children's rights to public attention is child abuse, particularly through the setting up of ChildLine and the highly publicised cases of abuse of children in care. Children cared for by the social work departments are now better informed and able to exercise their rights by means of charters and procedures which seek to ensure they have been consulted. Several local authorities now also employ a Children's Rights Officer and Lothian Council introduced a Children's Rights Charter which applied to all children living in the region. Although a degree of consensus now exists among many professionals about the importance of children's rights, many differences remain about how these should be defined and operationalised.

Understanding of children's rights

Though there was discussion throughout our interviews about children being protected, about their needs being met and about them being given choices e.g. about what they ate, what clothes they wore and how they spent their spare time, 'children's rights' as such were never mentioned explicitly by parents unless prompted. Evidently this was not a way of thinking or talking about children and family life which came naturally to them. When specifically asked whether they were aware of these developments and how they thought they might affect them, parents indicated some reluctance to think of their relationships with their children in terms of rights, preferring the needs based language and approach which they spontaneously adopted.

Similarly children seldom talked in terms of having 'rights' in relation to their parents, though their views of good parenting did incorporate key elements of a rights-based approach. They expected to be cared for, to be listened to and to have their point of view taken into account. They wanted to be treated fairly but many recognised that acting in children's best interests did not always equate with granting their every wish. The children's responses were thus consistent with the principles of children's rights but, since they were not specifically asked about this topic, the focus here is primarily on the views of parents.

While the majority of parents had heard of rights for children and had some understanding of what this might entail, this was usually confined to one aspect. Most commonly parents thought of the idea that their children had a right not to be smacked. Several parents thought that hitting children had already been made illegal or that legislation to that effect was in the pipeline, many having been informed about this from their own children. Thus typical responses on being asked what they knew about children's rights included:

> The only one we get — the kids are quite funny sometimes, they'll say 'You're not allowed to hit me, I'll phone up ChildLine'. And I'll say 'I'll phone up Parent line'.

> The only thing I'm aware of is they tried to ban parents smacking their children and in fact it is frowned upon isn't it, but I am not aware of anything else.

> He'll jail me if I touch him — I've had that from him as well — I think it's trying to bring in a law that you're not allowed to skelp your children.

> No I don't really know much about that at all. I know there's a law that they are bringing in about not smacking and things like that but I don't really know much about it.

> Children's rights are they that, if you hit a child, who is it they phone? Esther Rantzen … ChildLine!

Thus children's rights were framed not only in relation to one specific issue, but also in terms of children seeking external intervention against parents.

The second most common response was to refer to participative rights, i.e. children having a say and being able to influence what happened in their lives. Several parents spoke of children 'divorcing' their parents, reflecting the terminology used in the media. Responses to the initial question about whether they were aware of recent developments in children's rights included:

> Does that mean divorcing their parents?

> Yes about divorcing parents and all sorts of things.

> I don't really know, I do remember the American thing, divorce the parents … and obviously now children can't be punished at school?

> It's an issue for my eldest child. I mean, in quotes 'I'm nearly 16 and you can't do this to me and you can't say that to me, and you can't make me do this'. But I think that's a lot of hype he's picked up from his friends.

> They have the right to say 'no', he has the right to make up his own mind, make his own choices, his own decision and he's got the right to voice his own opinion or whatever without feeling bad or guilty.

Interestly most comments about children deciding with whom they would live came from single parents.

The group of foster carers were the only people who referred initially to provision rights:

> I heard something about children and how much pocket money they should get — Well basically to me a child's right is to be loved, is to be kept warm and fed and to be taught the everyday things in life.

Other foster carers referred to children's right to information about their personal history and the options available to them. People in touch with social work services, including foster carers, adopters and parents attending self-help groups appeared to be generally better informed about children's rights than other parents. An adoptive parent referred to the following:

> They have the right to feel secure and safe within their environment and I think they have the right to make decisions, informed decisions themselves appropriate to their age. I think they have the right to a certain degree of independence. They have to the right to feel, to be able to realise their potential whatever that means without coming under pressure.

The above quote is also one of the few examples where parents talked about children's rights as something they themselves had incorporated and believed in, whereas most portrayed it as an idea from elsewhere, predominantly the law, the media, professionals.

Parents' attitudes towards children's rights

Unlike many of the other topics we discussed, parents were not always clear about where they stood on children's rights. Indeed since their understanding was usually partial, they were sometimes working out their attitudes in the course of the interview. A number pointed out that children were often not treated fairly or with respect by other adults. Examples included being ignored when waiting to be served in shops, being rudely moved on when out playing and having their views ignored within the school system.

Not surprisingly, parents' attitudes towards children's rights reflected their views of children. Parents who emphasised the competence of children were more comfortable with the concept of rights than parents who thought children needed a lot of guidance and control. Attitudes to rights were also linked to perceptions of the role of parents. Some parents took the view that the majority of parents acted in the best interests of their own children most of the time and consequently could be trusted to make decisions on their behalf. Others emphasised parents' fallibility and the potential for abusing parental power, in which case children were thought to need separate rights and access to other sources of support. Two mothers pointed out that parents did not 'own' their children but had them in 'trust'. A mother and father within the same family might have different attitudes, as one person illustrated, comparing her attitude and her husband's:

> Well, I think children have an opinion of their own as well and I do think children should be able to voice their opinions and I do think they should be classed as individuals as well. I mean, I think children should have a right to say or do, if they feel it's right, say out in a crowd what's right. Whereas I feel he thinks the children should be seen and not heard. But I don't think that way about children. I think they are individuals and if they have anything to say to you then they should be able to say it without being condemned before they have even opened their mouths. I do think they should have a right to say what they feel. And they should be allowed to do what they think is right if it's not too outrageous.

It was not possible to make a simple classification on whether parents viewed children's rights positively or negatively, partly since people's understanding of what was meant by children's rights was so variable and since an individual might be in agreement with one aspect, such as protection, and not another, such as participation.

It also emerged that unease with the terminology and language of rights could co-exist with real commitment to protecting children and giving them as much of a say in their life as possible. A number of parents were unconvinced that charters and legal requirements would achieve a better deal for children and thought it might adversely affect the nature of the parent–child relationship. One of the adoptive mothers put forward this argument in the following terms:

> I think that children should have rights. I think what's happened is they're trying to lay it down in charters. I don't know that that's the right way to do it, I don't think that's the way to get children rights ... I think it, it maybe politicises it a little, it can change the relationship between child and parent ... I think any good parent accepts that their child is a person first, not a thing that just happens to be under your power, smaller than you are. So you have to respect that individual like you would respect any other individual, you don't need a charter to do that. To be aware that other people have needs and other people have the right to certain, the right to space and the right to be able to develop and the right to have their own opinions ... But I think if you set it down in a charter, I think it puts parents on their guard, it makes them defensive, they feel like they're being questioned in some way and that there's this sort of power balance between parent and child being affected and that in some ways their rights as parents has been sort of devolved, you know affected, and I think it can give children the wrong message in that it can give them the idea that their parents are not up to the job or they have rights independently, just because they're children. I think it's a two-way

thing, this idea of respecting other people's wishes and realising other people's needs, I think it's important that children realise at an early age if at all possible that adults have needs as well and that parents have needs. And so I think laying it all down, it's sort of, it turns it into a power battle, it doesn't have to be. It should be a reciprocal thing.

The above has been reproduced at some length because it reflects some common themes in the views parents expressed. Several parents spoke about the reciprocity between children's rights and responsibilities and believed that, by emphasising 'rights', the notion of corresponding responsibilities was undermined. Others took the view that respecting children, treating them as individuals and giving them some say in family decisions was an inherent part of good parenting. However, they conceived this in terms of 'natural justice' or responding to children's 'needs' and were uncomfortable with the thought of parents being subject to charters and legal requirements. These were seen as both unnecessary and ineffective: unnecessary for parents who 'naturally' accorded their children respect and ineffective in forcing others to do so.

One of the foster carers clearly voiced these sentiments:

I think all children not just foster children should be aware of how old it is when they can go to a GP on their own and what they can do, when and where, that even in your own family when you get to a certain age you know you should have the right to privacy and things like that, not 'this is my right, give it to me', but about the respect as they grow and change, and for children … to me, it's sort of natural that children should be respected as they are growing up. I know it's not that way for other people, I don't know what makes them like that, I don't know that you can impose things on them, say 'look at this sort of age this is what you should be doing for your children', or whether it's that more general education of the public into sort of awareness of children and the way they treat them, they respect them.

In common with the adoptive mother quoted earlier, this foster carer was well informed and broadly in favour of children having rights, yet both were cautious about endorsing an approach which was legalistic and emphasised 'rights' rather than 'needs' and respect. Conferring rights was seen as a process, the product of particular attitudes, rather than behaviour which could be enforced by law.

The rural parents were also wary of formally giving children 'rights' but thought that in practice they did treat their children with respect and acted in their best interests:

I don't think it's good [that children are aware of their rights] at such a young age — But you do give them choices — You've got to negotiate with them otherwise I mean their lives would be miserable, I mean at the end of the day its their happiness that is paramount to you even through you won't let them do what they want to do … you're not just laying down the law — It's a case of persuading them that they're going to benefit and maybe going to enjoy it … Well I think any parent worth their salt would be doing that anyway; I don't think they need somebody laying it down in law.

Underlying this point of view is an assumption that 'good' parents would always act in their children's best interests. Parental power over children was seen as benign and proper so that attempts to reduce this were seen as potentially harmful for parents and children alike. Not everyone shared this positive view of parenthood, as one single mother's comments indicate:

> … sadism and bullying within parenthood is not unusual at all. It goes, I mean I see it all the time, and that's with people who are educated, financially well off, hold responsible positions.

The question of reducing parents' power was opened up by some foster carers who were able to draw on their experience of operating in a context where children's rights were made explicit:

> I am for giving them rights to a certain extent but not for taking the parents' away. Because I find that if you give the kids their rights, which they should be entitled to, you find that the parents are left in the cold then and you think, well, what else can I give them? You have given them all their kind of knowledge they should know. You sit and tell them 'this is your right and that's your right. You should have pocket money every week, and you should do what you're told and yes, you can get a row. No, I can't smack you'. These kind of things. When you sit and say that to them and then maybe if they really get your temper going and you go [shake fist], but you can't. 'That's my right', you know.

Several parents felt that giving children rights made life more difficult for them, pointing out that children were already demanding in response to television advertising and peer pressure. The thought of them being able to claim a specified amount of pocket money filled some parents with horror. Other parents worried that their children would be denied parental protection, for example if they could stay out as long at they wanted and go to bed when it suited them. Both groups who lived in city schemes (one of fathers, one of mothers) felt the 'official' line on 'no smacking' gave their children the upper hand. A number of parents wanted to confer rights when they considered their children were ready to exercise them responsibly and there was fear that emphasising rights without responsibilities would make children selfish. Giving children rights was sometimes equated with handing over total control.

The idea that their children could make a complaint against them was seen by some parents as laughable or outrageous, as indicated by some of the references to ChildLine quoted earlier. However parents often went on to qualify such a remark by saying that such services were necessary for abused, as opposed to well cared for children (such as their own). Children's rights were therefore seen as not universal but only necessary when parents failed to protect and care for children adequately. From this perspective, rights applied selectively to certain other parents, but did not have universal implications for parents like themselves. A couple from the city scheme expressed this point of view when explaining why the children's rights movement had had no impact on how they brought their children:

Mother: ... because our kids' rights are adhered to ...

Father: We've always given them rights, not given them rights but ...

Mother: We've always respected their rights because they have natural rights. Normally you don't abuse your children. You give them their say ...

Father: I think all these rights have developed out of the abuse of children. I mean they have been so abused. Children have been abused for so long that they have had to have rights imposed. I'm not talking about their 'normal' rights, that sort of right to have an opinion and things like that but for rights which are backed by law.

It seemed to several parents unnatural to give children rights. Rights were an imposition which well cared for children should not have to worry about. Similarly the group of foster carers considered foster children's knowledge of their rights and ability to negotiate with social workers a sign of their deprivation. Conferring rights was thought to rob children of their childhood innocence and 'right' to rely on adults to care for them.

Thus most parents' views were based on particular conceptions of children, families and society. Family relationships were largely seen as a private matter, which external intervention and especially the law was likely to harm rather than help. Parents were seen as those who generally know what is in their children's best interests, including when and how to consult them. Representatives of wider society only had a role in relation to a minority of abusive families who deviated from commonly accepted norms.

Parents' actions: provision, protection and participation

Although most parents were suspicious and critical of conceiving parent–child relationships within a rights discourse, and especially a legal rights context, their actions, as reported in previous chapters, demonstrated an implicit respect for children's rights to basic care and protection. All parents took it as self-evident that they would provide basic care for their children and help prepare them as well as possible for adult life. Parents also had a role in helping children access resources outwith the home such as clubs, medical services and, when problems arose, schools.

Most parents did not consider that smacking contravened children's rights. Numerous parents distinguished between smacking and abusing children, the one being seen as a component of good parenting, and the other unacceptable. As discussed elsewhere in the report, only a few parents said they did smack their children at this age but some liked to retain the threat. This was the majority view but a few parents were very much opposed to smacking and taught their children to assert themselves against any violation of their bodies or personal space.

In relation to participation, many parents gave children a choice about everyday matters such as what they ate, which clothes they wore or where the family went on holiday, though others took the view that because parents paid the bills, they should call the tune.

There was less inclination to allow children's views to influence major decisions such as whether the family should move house or with whom children should live when parents split up. Children aged eight to twelve were generally thought to have insufficient experience and understanding to make a considered judgement, though the value of consulting with them and keeping them informed was widely recognised.

Views were varied on whether more attention to children's rights had influenced how people brought up their children. The majority view was that it had made no difference, either because parents considered they already 'respected' their children or because they were adamant that they would continue to smack or be controlling because they believed this was the correct way to bring up their children. However a number of parents felt they would now be much less ready to smack their children in public and one woman thought that this trend is developing so that parents whose children are pre-school now are less likely to smack children at all.

Conclusions

In summary, most parents were not well informed about legal and professional conceptions of children's rights and viewed with some suspicion attempts to formalise them legally. Parents liked to remain in control and most parents saw this as being the best way to promote children's best interests. A few parents disagreed, believing that parents frequently abused their power over children and thus welcoming any source of redress children might have.

Although both parents' and children's notions about 'good parenting' incorporated many children's rights principles, they were more comfortable with an approach to parent–child relationships with emphasised the language of needs, as they perceived them, rather then rights.

Whilst most parents are uncertain about the meaning and relevance of children's rights, they know that changes are afoot and feel somewhat threatened by the term and some of the specific applications they have heard about. Parents have not been included in professional and academic thinking on this subject and many are learning from their children that they have 'rights'. If giving children rights is to improve their lives, it seems important that steps are taken to include parents in the debate. Parents do accept that children have certain moral rights to protection and participation, but are mostly sceptical about framing these in formal legal terms.

CHAPTER 10

Support for Parents: Shared Responsibility in Middle Childhood

Introduction

In the same way that parents seek to reach an appropriate balance between giving children freedom and keeping them safe, so the aim of government policy in relation to children is to ensure they are provided for and protected without undermining the parents' primary responsibility. In principle this is achieved by sharing the responsibility for bringing up children between parents and the state. As long as they meet basic requirements, for example by ensuring their children are properly educated and do not suffer unnecessary harm, parents have considerable scope to determine what is best for their children. At the same time a range of services are provided by statutory and voluntary agencies, both to support families and to protect children by intervening when parental behaviour seems to threaten their welfare (Hill *et al*. 1995). It has been argued that these professional services influence parents in subtle yet powerful ways, thus reducing their apparent autonomy (Parton 1991). The way in which responsibility for children is shared is therefore not straightforward, support and influence being inextricably linked.

The parents we met with talked about the kinds of support or services they would want at this middle stage. Reflecting the study's purpose, we specifically asked parents what kind of health education resources they would find most helpful. In addition parents made comments throughout the interviews about their contacts with services such as education and health. Based on these responses, this chapter highlights some aspects of the kind of support parents expect and receive from professional services.

Evidently, parental support and influence is not confined to formal services. Indeed, family, friends and other children's parents were seen as more important, as outlined in several earlier chapters. However it might be argued that access to professional information and services becomes increasingly important during middle childhood, as children begin to learn about aspects of life on which parents are not necessarily well informed.

Topics on which parents wanted information

Parents were asked to identify the topics on which they would want health education agencies to provide additional information or advice. 'Health education' had been broadly defined as promoting social and moral as well as physical well-being. The following issues were the most common ones volunteered by parents as ones they wanted to know more about:

- illegal drugs, smoking, alcohol
- puberty, telling children about sex, HIV and Aids; homosexuality
- empowering children to resist abusive behaviour
- controlling unruly children
- impact of adolescence
- how to listen to children
- children's needs for care and attention
- children's rights
- racism.

By far the most frequent request was for information on drugs. Parents were keenly aware of their ignorance of drugs and this contributed to their sense of inadequacy and powerlessness when discussing the issue with their children. Information on sex, HIV and Aids was also frequently requested. However parents also wanted to learn more about managing the everyday aspects of growing through this stage, focusing for example on the particular needs of children during this transitional stage and how to listen to children effectively.

Though there was a wish for accurate factual information, parents also wanted advice on how best to use this knowledge, how to impart it to their children and how to influence their behaviour. Some parents found it very difficult to talk to their children about drugs and sex and a few parents raised particular worries about how to respond if a child is gay. In general parents wanted both knowledge and the skills to deploy this effectively.

As we saw in Chapter 9, some parents were concerned about how to reconcile ideas about children's rights with their wish to protect their children and act in their best interests. Perhaps in consequence of these issues having been raised, a number of parents requested information about what was meant by children's rights and the ways in which parents were expected to take them into account.

The suggestion that racism should be included came only from a few suburban parents who knew friends or colleagues who had experienced racist treatment. They thought parents needed to recognise the existence of racism and to learn how to help children live without prejudice in a multicultural society. Their view that many parents living in predominantly white areas were unaware of this issue was to some extent borne out by the fact that it was raised in so few discussions. A broader based survey commissioned by NCH highlighted much more widespread concern about racism among parents and children (NCH 1997).

Methods of providing information

In general, there was broad agreement among parents on what topics should be included in a health education programme for parents. There was however less unanimity about how the relevant information and advice would best be disseminated. While some people wanted written material they could dip into as required, others preferred to be more actively involved, for example through helping children make sense of health education programmes at school or receiving personal advice from experts on specific issues. Some people wanted information from professionals but not advice. They pointed out that opinions about child care practices tend to change over time and that an approach which suits one family may be unsuitable for another. Indications were that a mix of approaches were needed, both to cater for parents' different styles and to help ensure that complex messages were not over-simplified.

Irrespective of the kind of information they wanted, there was widespread agreement that parents did not at present know where to access the kind of information they wanted. Generally well-informed parents who were well versed in the use of libraries and information technology pointed out themselves that, despite wanting to be more informed about drug use among young people, they had not in fact located any suitable material. Similarly parents knew very little about local services and did not know where to locate help for a particular problem. The NCH Family Forum survey also reported that over half of parents did not know where to get help with problems such as drug and alcohol misuse and violence at home (NCH 1997).

In terms of written information, posters were generally dismissed as unsuitable for conveying complex messages. Similar criticisms were made of leaflets, which many parents said they ignored. However other people thought widely distributed leaflets could helpfully heighten awareness of issues and convey basic information. There was a suggestion that a book covering a range of topics in some detail would be appropriate. This would include such topics as puberty, children's rights and information about services. One mother pointed out that parents found books on caring for babies helpful and the same should apply to older children. It was proposed that this would include such topics as puberty, children's rights and information about services. Another parent took this idea further, suggesting that the book for parents could be designed in conjunction with the health education programme in schools. Her idea was that parents would be able to read up on a topic which was being taught in school at the same time.

Television was seen as a particularly powerful source of information, both through factual programme such as news items and documentaries and through introducing relevant storylines on soaps. Several parents commented on the strong influence which television and advertising had on children, suggesting that programme makers could support parents by conveying responsible messages or make life more difficult by encouraging rebellion. One of the advantages of television is that parents and children can view together and several parents wanted health education resources specifically to encourage interaction between parents and children.

There were many calls for schools and parents to work much more closely together and some parents complained that they knew very little of what was being taught in terms of health or social education. While some people wanted written material, others would have preferred a talk from an expert on specific topics. We were told about one primary school which had organised a very successful programme on sex education. The classes took place in the evenings and were attended by parents and their eleven- to twelve-year-old children together. This kind of session was seen as helpful because it helped open up discussion of difficult topics between parents and children, while providing accurate information and an opportunity for discussion with someone well-informed on particular issues.

A number of parents pointed out contradictions between what was formally taught by teachers about personal, social and health education and the kinds of behaviour and eating habits schools appeared to encourage through other activities. In particular, some schools were thought to give little priority to sports and exercise, whilst the sale of 'junk' food was perceived to run counter to teaching in class about diet. Here again was an issue where parents emphasised what they saw as children's best interests as regards health and diet, disapproving of children having the opportunity to have too much choice in what they ate and drank.

Many parents were keen to have a dialogue with the professionals rather than to be passive recipients of information and guidance. While they welcomed access to knowledge expertise, they also made critical judgements about whether general advice suited their family's particular circumstances.

Services for children and support to parents

School staff were generally viewed as important players in bringing up children. School was where children spent a large part of each day. While most parents were pleased with how their children were being educated, many would have liked to work more closely with school staff.

In addition to wanting to be more informed about or involved in social and health education sessions, a number of parents would have liked more say in non-educational matters affecting their children. Matters of diet and exercise were again to the fore. Parents identified a number of ways in which schools could detract from what parents saw as their own more positive influence. Tuck-shops sold sweets and sugary drinks rather than more wholesome alternatives, school lunches lacked nutrition and boring PE classes quashed enthusiasm for exercise. The following was typical of several comments:

> When I worked in school dinners it was all prepacked things and hot dogs and sausage rolls ... School dinners are definitely not the same as they used to be, I don't think. They say the nutrition is still there ... but I don't think so.

There seemed to be no routine opportunity for parents and staff to discuss these kinds of issues together. Only parents in the rural village, where the school was an important centre of community life, indicated that they had a say in matters such as whether children routinely brushed their teeth at school or were served sugary drinks at intervals.

Even when it came to involving parents in school life, it seemed the format and focus was determined by staff. One woman would have welcomed an opportunity to join in some activities with her children but the school's way of promoting parental involvement was to provide a room where parents could meet socially, sometimes with input from school staff or health visitors. This mother had expressed her point of view to school staff but resignedly accepted that the school policy was determined by other people and considerations:

> I have asked the school. If they have a link up room which is for parents only, which I don't see the point of, if the children cannot be present. [At my sister's children's school] her children are allowed in to the room at lunch-times and play computer and tapes and things. You know my sister can sort of also join in with their education for that part and learn just what they are doing for the day. But they don't do it on this side [of the city], in this area.

While it was not easy for parents to make suggestions to schools, it was quite common for schools to recommend particular courses of action to parents. As noted in the introduction to this chapter, services for children also perform a monitoring function to ensure that children in need of care and protection are identified. A number of the parents, from a range of social backgrounds, were aware of this element which was clearly articulated by a group of suburban mothers:

> There's lots of different ways of being a parent now, all of them are quite acceptable, but there's a lot more rules on how to be a parent as well, so that makes it, although you can do lots of different parenting, you are being more closely watched by the school and by the GP. I'm not saying that makes it difficult but it's something that you're quite conscious of, that you're not totally unobserved, that there is a presence — There is almost like performance indicators, you know, within the school and with the GP, that you have to match up to, and you're aware that they are there ... — If the children deviate from what seems to be a fairly tight band of norm you're offered support which starts you panicking. Well one of my kids once took a 'maddie' in the school — just, [said] 'I've had enough, this is it, I'm leaving'. And I was called up and I was offered the opportunity to take her to an educational psychologist. [It was] one episode, never again happened, only happened the once, but I came away and I actually phoned up a friend who deals with children with learning difficulties to see, 'Have I missed something?' and it took me a long time to get over the concern I felt.

Parents thus did not always see offers of help in relation to problems with children as supportive. However other parents, mostly from the city schemes, were coping with very difficult behaviour from children and would have appreciated some advice on how to manage this. While some would have liked a non-stigmatised advice service to be provided by the school nurse or health visitor, others preferred the idea of an informal service manned by other parents. Reassurance that some problems were normal was experienced as enormously supportive:

> There are pressures on me from everywhere to be a good parent, just from everywhere, from telly, from anything you pick up from other people's conversations — You're always quite reassured if you meet someone and they're saying my children are driving me round the bend — You tend to think 'where am I going wrong?' — Yes but everybody else is in the same boat.

The idea of a helpline for parents was also proposed but there were different views about whether a service of this kind should be run by parents or professionals.

Mistrust of professional judgement was also clearly expressed by a group of mothers from a city scheme. They believed that, in an area where reluctance to fight was viewed as a sign of weakness, a school rule requiring their children to report bullying to staff rather than hit back was inappropriate. They accepted that resolving differences by negotiation was preferable but did not believe that this strategy could be applied in their particular situation:

> That's the only thing I don't agree with in this school, is about this conduct rule, they're no allowed to hit back and he gets himself into a state and I'm like that 'I don't give a damn what anybody says, if anybody hits you, you hit them back and I'll speak to the teacher' — They've got to, see if they don't they're going to get it non-stop — They're going to be picked on all their lives.

This conversation highlights how some parents felt out of step with professional opinion and that much more dialogue is needed if parents and professionals are to work in partnership. Whether in relation to specific issues such as the fare sold in tuck-shops or on more abstract questions such as policy on bullying and children's rights, many parents felt excluded from professional decision making and debate. Consequently, children can be given conflicting messages, while parents may be somewhat reluctant to accept official advice on what is best for their children or to seek help when it is needed.

Wider responsibilities

When asked what kind of support parents bringing up children needed, the most frequent request was for good quality services. Parents wanted a well resourced education and health service and ready access to affordable leisure activities. Many were not convinced that providing more advice or information for parents was the most effective way of improving children's lives. Instead they pointed out the adverse effects of factors beyond most parents' control such as living on a low income or in areas with poor air quality or where drug use and crime are common.

Parents looked for people with influence in society to highlight practices which placed children at risk and to take steps to counteract them. There were suggestions that the police should target shopkeepers who sell cigarettes or solvents to young people and that politicians and church leaders should lead the fight against drugs.

When it came to life within the family, many parents felt under pressure to perform well, both as a parent and provider for the family. Trying to live up to ideals presented by television and advertising and fears about insecure or no employment fuelled the tensions, so that parents were in fact less able to be the supportive and attentive carers they aspired to be.

Summary

Parents were very willing to accept responsibility for their children's up-bringing but expected to be provided with the resources they needed to carry out this demanding task. The key elements they sought were:

- accurate information on key topics, presented in a range of formats to suit parents' different styles of learning and lifestyles
- consultation and closer involvement with schools and other professionals working with children
- good quality universal and specialist support services
- a safe and healthy environment.

The key message from parents was that services to support children's up-bringing would only be effective if they took account of the realities of life outwith and within the family and were based on consultation and dialogue with parents.

CHAPTER 11

Other Research on Middle Childhood

In the previous chapters we have made occasional reference to other writers' ideas and research findings in relation to middle childhood, but we have deliberately kept these to a minimum, so that the quotations and messages of our own studies could be presented in a lucid way. Now it is time to examine the broader context of academic and professional conclusions which have been drawn about this period in the life span. Although the two studies described thus far were wide-ranging in subject matter and based on a reasonable cross-section of the relevant population, nonetheless there were limitations of geography, scale and focus. This chapter gives us a chance to assess how far the work of others supports, amplifies, qualifies or even contradicts what we found from our samples of children and parents.

Potentially a vast amount of writing is relevant to this topic, so this review has to be selective. We discuss first, theoretical approaches. The main part of the chapter then considers wider evidence about the themes which have been covered in earlier chapters. We shall give particular attention to those which record the everyday experience of parents and children. Such naturalist and consumer accounts are surprisingly rare in the academic psychological literature, which has tended to concentrate on controlled circumstances and abstracted variables in order to identify correlations and test theoretical concepts (Hogan 1998; Richards and Morrow 1996).

Theorising middle childhood

Two views

Mid-childhood can be seen as the main arena in which an intellectual battle is currently being fought. On one side is the perspective of traditional developmental child psychology. This presents children's development as following fairly well-defined paths along a range of dimensions: physical, intellectual and psycho-social. Whilst recognising individual and group diff-erences as important, this viewpoint portrays most children as passing through typical 'stages' in which certain features predominate. Each stage is seen as forming a foundation on which subsequent stages are built. Children are working towards achieving their full potential in adulthood. Although the timing and duration of children's passage through particular stages will vary considerably, in part due to environmental influences, nevertheless most eight-to nine-year-olds are perceived as having much in common which diff-erentiates them from most children who are a few years younger or older.

On the other side of the debate is the newly but rapidly emerging sociology of childhood, which also draws on historical and anthropological accounts (Hutchby and Moran-Ellis 1998; Mayall 1994b; Qvortrup 1994). This per-spective has mounted a critique of what it regards as the universalist assumptions of conventional developmental psychology and the implicit dev-aluing of children by representing them as deficient adults. An alternative view is put forward which emphasises that the nature of childhood is variously con-structed according to the beliefs and values of particular times and societies through changing interactive processes. This notion was put forward most strikingly by Ariès (1971) in arguing that Medieval society had no concept of childhood (at least after infancy) since the activities, expectations and dress of the children and adults were the same. A second strand to recent sociological thinking is that due recognition should be given to children as 'competent actors'. In other words, they are actively involved in creating the worlds they live in, not simply passive recipients of adult socialisation or biological imp-eratives.

We now consider each of these approaches in more detail.

Developmental psychology and middle childhood

The most influential models of childhood stages were devised many years ago, but remain influential in writing and teaching. Even though criticised and modified within psychology itself (Burman 1994; Morss 1996), the ideas continue to be widely used in both textbooks and research. They are prominent in much professional training. The first type of stage theory concentrates on relationships; the second type focuses on intellectual development. It should be noted that all the theories are rooted in European and North American patterns of social relationships and schooling, though a limited amount of cross-cultural testing has occurred.

The earliest of the classical stage theories is that of Freud. He suggested that young children pass through three phases of psycho-sexual development – oral, anal and genital (Gardner 1994). This was followed by the 'latency' period of middle childhood in which it was thought that not much happened until puberty burst on the scene. 'Freud called this the latency period as if it were a period of waiting, with nothing very important happening. In one sense he was right: it appears to be a relatively calm period. But there is a great deal of change nevertheless' (Bee 1989, p.552).

Erikson (1965) developed a more rounded psycho-social theory which encompassed emotional and social as well as sexual development. Like Freud, though, he saw early childhood as a busy period in which positive care led to important achievements – trust, autonomy and initiative. Poor care could result in the opposites of mistrust, doubt and guilt. Whereas according to Erikson the first five years of life encompassed three stages, the next eight or so years from about five to thirteen constituted a single phrase characterised by 'industry' in school and elsewhere. As Fahlberg (1982) put it 'the primary task of the child between six and ten is to master the problems he encounters outside the family unit' (p.58). Fahlberg names several qualities she saw as typical (one might say stereotypical) of the nine to ten-year-old – busy, liking routines, subject to only short-lived emotional shifts, relaxed, dependable. Erikson emphasised the importance of interaction with peers and teachers for establishing a foundation not only for learning but for self-worth. Most children develop a positive sense of self-worth, but for those who fail in school or who are isolated or rejected, a sense of inferiority results (Asher and Coie 1991; LeFrancois 1990).

Attachment theory is also in the broad psycho-social tradition of Freud and Erikson, with an emphasis on the crucial importance of early relationships between children and parents (Bowlby 1969; Holmes 1993). The core idea is that unloving or inconsistent care leads to insecurity, which tends to generalise to other relationships. Children with loving, responsive parents or carers have a 'secure base' which gives them confidence in wider social interactions. By contrast, children who have experienced harsh or markedly inconsistent care develop mind-sets in which they expect rejection and find it hard to trust others (Rutter and Rutter 1993). In its early formulation, attachment theory posited that children who had not formed close relationships with parental figures before the age of two to three were virtually 'doomed for life'. It is now recognised that children who have experienced early emotional deprivation can recover and make significant attachments after the age of five, though this is not easy after long and severe experiences of affectionless care (Howe 1996; Schaffer 1990).

Taken together these influential models suggest that for most children the primary school years form a period of relative quiet and a focus on practical actions. The physical body apparently takes a back seat. Whereas young children and adolescents are seen as very occupied with their internal bodily sensations, the five- to twelve-year-old's body has little emotional significance and is mainly a vehicle for mobility and activity. By five, most children are thought to have gained control of sensual, eating and defecatory activities and their associated feelings. The sexual impulses of puberty remain a long way off. By implication, parenting issues too are largely dormant in this period. Provided parents have dealt well with the needs and demands of their infant children, then their children have the trust and security to concentrate in an untroubled way on school and leisure.

Whereas the theories mentioned so far focused on relationships with other people (particularly parents), Piaget's stage theories dealt with the intellectual development of children. In contrast to some of the more passive conceptions of children's developments put forward by his contemporaries, Piaget depicted children as actively engaging with their physical and social environments to develop progressively more sophisticated and accurate representations of the world and of causal relations within it. For Piaget, children of about seven to twelve years were in what he called a 'concrete, operational stage.' They had moved beyond the intuitive and at times magical thinking of early childhood, when objects, events and relations were seen from a very 'ego-centric' view-point. In middle childhood, children are usually able to understand causes and effects in many immediate contexts, but find it hard to deal with abstract ideas and 'invisible' systemic relationships (like the 'economy' or algebra). They may still find it hard to distinguish fact and fantasy, genuine and dissembled emotions (Harris 1994; Williams, Wetton and Moon 1989). Among the accomplishments Piaget identified for this stage were: understanding that physical and mental operations are reversible; comprehension of classifications and hierarchies of phenomena (i.e. principles of inclusion and exclusion); and inductive logic (deriving principles from observations and experiences) (Bee 1995; Meadows 1990). By the age of eleven to twelve most children are able to solve problems systematically, monitor and adjust their own behaviour and organise complex tasks independently (Collings, Harris and Susman 1995).

Piaget's overall framework is still widely used in academic analyses (see e.g. Berti and Bombi 1988; Matthews 1992) and in schools (Smith and Cowie 1991). However, many of the details of his ideas have been modified or even overthrown by later investigations (Donaldson 1978; Cox 1980). According to Rutter and Rutter (1993) the notion of children as active agents in learning has stood the test of time, but the idea of invariant stages 'has turned out to be rather misleading' (p.193). Individual and cultural variations are much greater than Piaget acknowledged, whilst children's reasoning strategies are not uniform at any given age, but may take one of several forms depending on the context. Further, later research has shown that children's ability to understand phenomena ranging from chess to illness can be affected as much by their exposure to and hence knowledge of the specific subject as their age or general manner of intellectual competence (Bee 1992; Bluebond-Langner *et al.* 1990).

Piaget himself and Kohlberg (1969) applied a similar framework to consideration of moral judgements. For instance, pre-school children were portrayed as viewing rules as absolute. The wrongness of an act was mainly related to its effects regardless of whether a person meant to do it or it was an accident. By age nine to ten, children have come to see rules as more arbitrary and context-dependent, whilst moral opprobrium is now largely related to a person's intentions to cause harm or not. Doing good to others is regarded as either part of a fair exchange or, increasingly with age, related to personal loyalties or general moral injunctions.

It will be apparent already that there is no unified theory of child development. Moreover a number of recent writers have been more concerned to assess processes of development, behaviour or social interaction within particular domains of activity rather than to identify clear-cut stages (Bruner 1990; Parke 1989; Woodhead, Light and Carr 1991). In the last two decades developmental psychology has taken much greater account of the wider social environment. This has usually been within an ecological or systems framework (Bronfenbrenner 1979; Bee 1995). Whilst 'most researchers continue to endorse the basic tenets of developmentalism' (Woodhead 1997, p.78), much closer attention is paid to the cultural context which shapes children's particular behaviours and needs.

The sociology of childhood

For much of its history, sociology has not had a great deal to say about pre-teen children (Adler and Adler 1986), except as the products of different forms of socialisation, especially linked to ideas of culture and social class. This is rapidly changing and in the 1990s a number of sociologists have posed an academic challenge both to their own discipline and to conventional psychological accounts of childhood (Qvortrup *et al.* 1994). To caricature somewhat, psychology has seen children as following a set of largely universal pathways, though with significant variations related to individual differences and environmental and cultural influences. Sociologists, by contrast, emphasise that concepts of childhood in general and the particular experiences of children are 'social constructs'. In other words they are not universal givens, but are produced through social interpretation and interaction within particular social and historical contexts. This stress on the active creation of developmental experiences contingent on particular settings of social interaction is also gaining ground among a minority of psychologists (Sommer 1998).

Furthermore adults are not simply neutral observers of children's un-ravelling development, but have power over children and regard them through an adult-oriented lens. Conventional developmental accounts can be seen as devaluing children's own viewpoints, by treating them as 'human- becomings' rather than human beings (Shamgar-Handelman 1994). Hence, any attempt to understand children should include attention to adult preconceptions and interests, just as furtherance of children's rights challenges adult attitudes and behaviour. At this point, academic approaches to childhood link with policy analyses focusing on notions of children's rights. Children are seen as a marginalised social group denied social and political rights by adults and hence vulnerable to physical and sexual abuse and other forms of exploitation (Boyden 1997; Jenks 1996; Scraton 1997). Whereas children's lack of competence and heightened vulnerability compared with adults are con-ventionally used as reasons to exclude children from decision making even in the settings like schools in which they are centrally engaged, the rights perspective sees greater participation by children as necessary for their own protection.

An important element of the (relatively) new thinking is to stress that children themselves are active agents in the creation of their own social worlds (Mayall 1994a). There is some overlap here with the transactional view of development which has been influential in psychology for some time (Sameroff 1976), but sociologists are more concerned with current meanings of exp-eriences for children rather than the interplay of quantified variables (Qvortrup 1994). At the same time, it is noted that children's lives have become progressively organised (by adults) in formal settings like schools, uniformed organisations and activity clubs, leaving less scope than formerly for children to determine their own social worlds (Brannen and O'Brien 1996; Ennew 1994; Shamgar-Handelman 1994).

A further 'anti-developmental' argument is that children's thoughts, be-haviour and attitudes should be recognised as competent and relevant to their own situation, not merely as underdeveloped precursors of adulthood. In particular the 'stage' notion has been rejected and at times this has led to a somewhat disingenuous treatment of children and childhood as lacking any age or physical dimension. It is now being recognised that these cannot be ignored, but that their significance can be conceptualised in new ways (James and Prout 1997).

Interestingly, much of the research carried out under the auspices of the sociology of childhood (not all of it by sociologists!) has tended to focus on the middle period of childhood, since it is here that 'developmentalism' can be seen to have its greatest limitations and it is here therefore that most scope may exist for new insights. It is hard to deny the limited autonomy of babies and toddlers, though psychologists too nowadays recognise that infants have many comm-unicative and other abilities which were previously underrated and may 'control' social interaction as much as adults (Dunn 1993). Developmental psychologists recognise that teenagers have similar capabilities to adults. Sociology has a healthy tradition of youth studies, so that it is the primary school period which offers the most fertile ground for innovatory under-standing and analysis.

This approach rightly informs us of the diversity and complexity of children's experiences. It supports a constant questioning of adult assumptions about children and of adult–child interactions. Nevertheless immersion in the particulars of individual children needs to be set alongside evidence about structured inequalities based on material circumstances, gender, ability and so on. Physical and cognitive changes with age do not follow invariant sequences regardless of social and cultural influences, but equally 'experiences of child-hood, different and variable though these undoubtedly are and have been, are still lived out in a physical body' (Gittins 1998, p.45).

Links with the studies reported in this book

The two studies at the heart of this book had pragmatic aims and were not intended to apply or develop theory. There were carried out on the assumption that it is valuable to understand the perspectives of 'lay people' themselves, that is, ordinary members of the public, with respect to health education issues (Backett 1992; Hogg, Barker and McGuire 1996; Nettleton and Bunton 1995). As such they were in keeping with the current sociological emphasis on qualitative reporting and interpretation of participants and especially child-ren's experiences. Our presentation has inevitably mediated what children and parents said, but the methods of data gathering sought to maximise part-icipants' input into both the agenda and the summarising of issues, whilst our interpretation of the findings has sought to remain faithful to the meanings and priorities they expressed. In this way it is hoped that children's (and parents') subjective accounts not only convey their views as important in their own right, but guard against oversimplification and stereotyping which can result from quantified work which reduces complex reality to detached variables. Within the limitations of our own adult perspectives, we have also tried to regard the accounts of both children and parents as valid and competent each in their own way. The children were able to tell us about the rich worlds they inhabit, much of the content of which is often beyond the horizon of adult awareness.

On the other hand insights from developmental psychology are relevant. Stage theories with presumed universal application are now seen as over-simplified by almost everyone, but broad progressions in physical development and intellectual understanding do undoubtedly occur, though with highly variable time scales and very different significance depending on the socio-cultural context. We also found certain changes with age which roughly fit those noted by psychologists (especially when our data on younger children aged five and seven was taken account of (see Hill, Laybourn and Borland 1995). These changes included increased significance of emotional relation-ships and move to greater cognisance of the wider world (see also Williams, Wetton and Moory 1989). Older children in our studies were more able to reflect and comment on their experiences and knowledge than young children.

The views of many of the children we spoke to supported to some degree the notion of middle childhood as a relatively stable period, but it must be remembered that for some children this can be a time of turmoil when their circumstances are changing and unreliable. This was borne out by some of the traumatic experiences recounted by children attending special projects in the Well-being study. Paradoxically, some of these same children were urging adults to display more of what psychologists have portrayed as 'adult' qualities, namely to see things more from others' viewpoints – in this case children's. Parents' own statements suggested that it was not uncommon for them to disregard or undervalue children's perspectives, because of their preocc-upations with their own concerns, though these were often aimed at their children's best interests as they interpreted them.

It was the parents' views which, with some exceptions, were most at odds with the conventional image of the primary-school child. They described parenting children of this age to be more challenging than usually depicted. This partly related to perceived characteristics of the children, but was also very much linked to outside influences. Peers and the media were thought to support undesirable activities, whilst the local environment was often seen as fraught with dangers. For this reason, parents portrayed their most prominent role at this stage as seeking to protect their children through controlling their use of time and space. A range of techniques were used to do this, including rule enforcement, negotiation, 'preventive' teaching and facilitation of children's own competence. By and large the children accepted their parents' rights of authority in these respects. This could be seen as a mutually satisfactory way of handling the vulnerability-autonomy dilemma which was portrayed as the key issue of this age. An alternative interpretation is of children brainwashed to accept adult-imposed organisation of their time and activities (Oldman 1994; Shamgar-Handelman 1994).

Children's perspectives on their everyday experiences

In this section we briefly review some of the key findings from research aimed to understand children's perspectives on the relationships and activities in their daily lives. Many of the studies have been informed by the two main perspectives outlined above.

Children's views of what a family is

Relatively few studies have asked pre-teen children for their views on family life. One way of assessing what children mean by their 'family' is to ask them to draw or list those people who belong to their family and then discuss the product. An early investigation by Piaget himself suggested an age-related progression from seeing family as based on co-residence at seven to eight, to focusing mainly on biological ties by eleven to twelve (cited in Newman, Roberts and Syre 1993).

More recent work provides some confirmation of such a progression but suggests that it is the emotional rather than biological relationships which are most prominent (Newman *et al.* 1993). On the whole it seems that children focus on the nuclear family (though this pattern might well be different for those of Asian backgrounds, for instance). Also in mid-childhood, inclusion is based on mixed criteria taking account of both co-residence and the emotional quality of relationships, with biological explanations sometimes playing a part too. An ethnographic study in London schools aimed to tap into images of family life among seven- to ten-year-olds (O'Brien, Alldred and Jones 1996). Although the drawings of their families by some children were confined to their own household, many others included non-resident kin, especially if the household was headed by a lone parent. Most of the children thought that couples even if married did not constitute a family unless they also had children. On the other hand, divorce was not thought to eliminate the sense of being a family: 'They're still a family, even if Mum and Dad split up, whatever' (ten-year-old, cited in O'Brien *et al.* 1996).

Discussion with the children showed that many felt some anxiety about the possibilities of losing their parents through divorce, separation or death. They tended to see the main options for children without parents to care for them as being either extended kin or an 'orphanage'. The children seemed well informed about their friends' family circumstances and were sometimes more up to date on household changes than the school records.

Other studies have similarly shown how experience of parental separation depends very much on the processes leading up to and following the event, whilst concern about possible separation can figure strongly in intact households. In a Finnish investigation, children living in lone-parent households spoke about their lives as essentially 'normal' and unproblematic (Alanen 1998). A small Norwegian study was carried out of children aged five to nineteen whose parents had separated or divorced. Nearly all included all the people they lived with including a step-parent, but also the non-resident parent (Levin 1995). Three patterns were apparent:

- a single integrated family
- two separate 'families' with the child belonging to both
- two separate 'families' with the child in the middle.

Segregation was not necessarily seen as hostile. As a twelve-year-old who drew such a pattern remarked: 'My parents are not really divorced, because they do not quarrel' (cited in Levin 1995, p.67).

This contrasts with an image produced by one child in our Well-being study who drew himself with a thick black line through the middle to portray his feelings of sadness at the family split. Butler and Williamson (1994) noted that children who witness frequent parental rows were worried that the family was likely to break up. Williams et al. (1989, p.41) reported that one of the key messages of ten- and eleven-year-olds was 'Our security is shaken by family rows: We feel separation from our parents deeply'. In the main it seems that it is overt conflict which has the most impact in situations of potential or actual separation and divorce (Amato and Keith 1991).

Children's views on the qualities of family life

Both our studies illustrated that primary-school children want and appreciate continued demonstrations of love by their parents and others. The great majority of children in a survey of eight- to fifteen-year-olds described how their parents demonstrated love towards them (Ghate and Daniels 1997). Eighty-two per cent of those aged eight to eleven reported physical affection (e.g. hugs or kisses). Indeed studies of adolescents show that they too value parental support and guidance, even though minor disputes are not uncommon (Coleman and Hendry 1990; Gordon and Grant 1996).

Most children tend to spend more time with their mothers than their fathers (Ghate and Daniels 1997). In the main, children see mothers as the adults chiefly responsible for their health and well-being, though at primary age children themselves accept increasing responsibility (Mayall 1993). Usually, mothers are more actively engaged than fathers in discussions and arrangements about health-related issues (Brannen et al. 1994).

A survey of a representative sample of children in England and Wales concluded as we did that children were by and large accepting of parental controls, though they disliked certain kinds of punishment, especially beatings. Most said they expected when they become adults to be 'as strict' as their own parents. Likewise, the majority said they were content with their current level of independence and only one child in eight said they would like more say in things at home (Ghate and Daniels 1997).

Lindon explored with some groups of school children aged from eight years upwards their perspectives on family life and growing independence. Even allowing for the fact that she spoke with many teenagers as well as primary-school children, her conclusions were somewhat different from ours, which may reflect types of children seen, the questions asked or the manner of asking. Children in her study recognised that they are given or take more responsibility for self-care and for looking after their own domains than when younger:

> You have to look after things for yourself. Your parents don't do this any more. You have to change your clothes and get dressed. You have to do it all now.

> More is expected of you now. Like I have to tidy my room. (cited in Lindon 1996; all the quotes used here come from ten- to twelve- year-olds)

Some think they are more capable than parents give them credit for:

> They should trust you but they're expecting you'll mess it up. Like if it's something big or important like a video recorder. They think you'll drop it but I think I can do it. (cited in Lindon 1996)

Several made pleas to be allowed more opportunities and given more trust, acknowledging that they might not always get things right:

> Parents try to protect you and try to stop you making the same mistakes as them. But you have to learn by your own mistakes, not somebody else's.

> They worry about you getting into trouble. But that shows that they don't trust you. It's important that they trust you. (cited in Lindon 1996)

Correlational research within the developmental paradigm has examined the impact of certain categories of family form or parenting style on child outcomes, usually assessed in terms of emotional adjustment or educational progress. Various studies have indicated that firm, confident and loving parents tend to rear children who are happier and more socially adept than parents who are rigid or indulgent (Maccoby and Martin 1983). Without denying the validity of such generalisations, researchers who listen to children's own accounts of family life identify a complex tapestry of activities and feelings which are not readily predictable. 'Living in a certain type of family does not imply a certain kind of childhood' (Moore, Sixsmith and Knowles 1996, p.3). Moreover, children have active ways of coping with stresses and responsibilities, so that situations which adults may see as problematic like having a divorced or disabled parent can be experienced positively by children themselves.

Children's concerns, worries and fears

Age-related patterns have been identified in relation to the expression and identification of emotions, which can be linked to both cognitive and psychosocial development. Children aged five to eight have a more restricted vocabulary of usage and recognition than nine- to eleven-year-olds, more of whom are beginning to grasp more abstract terms and phrases which are necessary to analyse emotions. Children's emotional reactions tend to become self-conscious as they grow older (Harris 1992). They are increasingly affected by beliefs and assumptions about whether experiences 'should' be positive or negative (Aldgate 1988). During the primary-school years children develop their abilities to reflect on and monitor emotions, recognise ambivalence and differentiate situational influences (Meadows 1990). Middle childhood is also the time when children understand better the less immediate antecedents and repercussions of emotions, although there are marked individual variations (Terwogt and Harris 1993).

Rutter and Rutter (1993) concluded from studies largely based on adult reports and observations that by middle childhood most children have left behind the typical fears and anxieties of the pre-school years (e.g. in relation to separation, the dark, imaginary creatures). Others remain quite common (e.g. fear of snakes), whilst some are specific to children with certain temperaments (e.g. fear of meeting people). In general, short-term separations are managed more readily than when younger, but reaction to the death of a parent or other close relative is likely to be more intense and prolonged (Garmezy and Rutter 1983).

Our study noted that children had concerns which adults were thought to underestimate. The survey of eight- to fifteen-year-olds mentioned above (Ghate and Daniels 1997) found that worries were common in middle childhood and, contrary to popular and academic images, more common than among adolescents. More than twice as many of the under-twelves were classified as 'anxious' on a composite scale (22%) than those aged twelve to fifteen (10%). This might however partly reflect differences in willingness to admit to anxieties.

A large American survey invited children to record the type and intensity of worries they had (Silverman, La Greca and Wasserstein 1995). The researchers chose the domains of experience which children were asked to comment on (like health, family, money, war), but within each area they were invited to say in their own words what their concerns were. The areas of worry reported by the largest numbers of children were health (their own and other people's), school and personal harm. On the other hand, the events or issues that children worried about most frequently were socially oriented, i.e. they concerned classmates, friends and family. As in our study these anxieties related to disruptions in relationships such as parental arguments or separations, and rejection, betrayal and scapegoating in relation to peers. Understandably, illness and death to relatives caused children most distress. British work has also shown that children's greatest anxieties focus on actual or potential loss of close family members, whether through death or separation (Butler and Williamson 1994; Williams et al. 1989). Bullying is also a major concern which we shall discuss further below (NCH 1997). Fears of imagined creatures (like ghosts) are common at least up to the age of ten, though children often prefer not to tell adults about this (Williams et al. 1989).

Thus it appears that when asked open-ended questions children at this age rarely mention concerns about sex, drugs, abuse or abduction which are prominent in many adult's minds. On the other hand, if presented with a list of such issues, children do admit that these are important, even though they are not amongst their principal everyday worries. For instance, children in Scottish primary schools were asked to judge the importance to them of knowledge about twelve topics on a checklist. Health and hygiene, drugs and smoking came out top (Devine 1995). Similarly high proportions of children in a large survey acknowledged concerns about drug and alcohol abuse as well as bullying, when prompted in a questionnaire (NCH 1997).

As our studies found, both children and parents place a great deal of trust in family members and other familiar people. In one way, this is good, since children's well-being and indeed the social fabric could be undermined by regular mistrust in close relationships. Yet this can mean that risks from familiar people are unrecognised. The 'Draw and Write' study found that the images of drug-takers and dealers held by eight- to ten-year-olds were typically of people with a bizarre appearance. They did not associate drugs with people they knew well or who led 'ordinary' lives, as many illegal drug-takers do (Williams et al. 1989). A study which used pictorial vignettes to assess children's willingness to accede to requests from adults found that they were generally very willing to do so. Children were more likely to comply with familiar people, but half of six- to eight-year-olds and over one-third of ten-year-olds said they would do as asked by a stranger (Moran *et al.* 1997).

Friendships, social activities and peer difficulties

Children's peer relationships and friendships have been much studied, mainly through observation and structured questioning. By middle childhood, children in Western societies generally have a well-developed sense of friends as being distinct from others they are acquainted with (Erwin 1992). Friendships tend to be quite narrowly age-graded, that is, they are mostly within a few months or at most a year or two of each other. This evidently reflects the fact that much time is spent in year cohorts at school or in organised groups. Nevertheless some children do have friends of quite different ages. Spending time together and shared interests are important features of friendship, but by nine to eleven years less tangible aspects are important. These include the sharing of intimacies, offering advice and support, and loyalty (Berndt 1986). Friends also know about and tolerate ups and downs: 'she never minds when I'm in a mood' (quoted in Williams *et al.* 1989, p.47).

Our studies highlighted the importance to children of peer disputes and disruptions to friendships. Observational research has examined some of the processes involved, although generally with little emphasis on the less visible feelings of being bereft or excluded. When friends do fall out they sometimes use standard mechanisms for seeking a reconciliation without either side losing face (Bigelow, Tesson and Lewko 1996; Miller 1993). Examples include an invitation to join in a game or showing a new possession. Friendships are located in a wider social network so that disagreements are often public. Other children may help patch things up or provide an alternative playmate (James 1993). As children grow older they generally become more able to sort out peer difficulties without adult intervention – and increasingly prefer to do so (Collings *et al.* 1995).

As our respondents reported, gender has an important influence on relationships. Most obviously, children at this age usually spend most of their time with others of the same sex. Typically girls spend more time with one or a few particular friends towards whom they have intense loyalty sometimes interspersed with sharp conflict, whereas boys tend to form larger but looser friendship groups. Girls' conversations give greater attention to feelings and relationships, whilst boys are more inclined to focus on activities and status issues (Archer 1992; Ganetz 1995; Hartup 1992; Waldrop and Halverson 1975). As a result disruptions of relationships tend to be more significant for females. James (1993, p.231) observed that boys' memberships of larger groupings meant that 'change in the group's personnel is less noticeable', but 'for girls, in contrast, the loss of a friend is always an event'.

The children in our studies indicated that teasing, insults and rejection were often based on physical and behavioural characteristics. This is confirmed in other research. Children with disabilities or of minority ethnic groups may be particularly susceptible:

> They think I am stupid.

> Enemies make fun of you because you are different. (quoted in Wade and Moore 1993, p.102)

Many children with learning difficulties who attend mainstream schools feel unhappy at break times, because they are isolated or picked on:

> Them kids give me battering playtimes.

> Get kicked in playtime. (cited in A. Lewis 1995)

Coie (1991) reported evidence that negative attitudes based on stereotyping (e.g. in relation to disability) may be defused or reinforced, depending on how a particular child responds. This should not be taken to mean that a victim of discrimination is responsible for the effects, but does mean a combined strategy of combating prejudice and adjusting self-presentation can be effective.

Bullying was a major concern of children in the Well-being study. Many children are anxious that they will be picked on when starting at secondary school:

> I get all sweaty when I think about going to comp. I get worried about getting picked on and coping socially. It'll probably be OK, but you still get worried. (cited in Butler and Williamson 1994, p.61)

Only in the last few years has this issue received concerted adult attention. Earlier views that it was just part of growing up or difficult to prevent have given way to whole school and whole community responses which Scandinavian experience has shown to be effective (Olweus 1991). Bullying is common, affecting about one child in six regularly. Verbal teasing is most common, but hitting, kicking and extortion affect significant numbers (Smith and Cowie 1991). Certain individuals are more prone to bully and, if unchecked, this can lead on to persistent abuse of power (Boulton 1995; Smith and Sharp 1994). Victims of bullying can become very depressed, lacking in confidence and unable to learn well at school. Verbal bullying is more common by and to girls, with physical bullying more prevalent among boys (Smith and Sharp 1994; Whitney and Smith 1993).

Much peer interaction is more positive than this, fortunately. The careful observation and recording of playground activities by Opie (1993) revealed a rich world, which adults once inhabited, but the details of which are often forgotten. The games, stories, songs, sayings and jokes described by the Opies represent a cultural heritage passed on from one generation to the next, with certain constant themes but also a rapid adaptability to social changes and recent events. These also illustrate vital mechanisms in which children learn about life, death, sex, current events and myriad other issues in ways mediated by their peer networks. Play in school breaks and after school is also a time when moral issues like fairness and the regulation of social interaction are explored and tested (Blatchford, Creeser and Mooney 1991; Hill and Tisdall 1997; Sluckin 1981).

Use of space

Children in rural areas talked to us about mainly enjoyable but occasionally frightening explorations of country lanes, open fields and woods. Urban children were more likely to describe walks through their neighbourhoods as *en route* to specific places, like school, a club or the shops. One of the parents' main worries was how to ensure that their children did not suffer accidents, abduction or assault when out on their own or with peers. Concerns about dangerous people and places in urban areas has been widely reported (Ward 1978). Research in Glasgow showed that parents were often acutely aware of local physical hazards like traffic and broken railings. Whereas professionals emphasised the need for parents and children to learn how to avoid such dangers, parents argued that a more desirable strategy was to make the actual environment safer (Roberts *et al.* 1995).

The notion of territorial range has been used to depict the area with which a child is familiar (Moore 1986). This normally increases with age and typically boys have a larger territorial range than girls of the same age (Katz 1993). A distinction may also be made between a permitted range of movement (alone or with friends) and the actual range, since children often venture further than their parents are aware (Hart 1979; McNeish and Roberts 1995). Children are usually able to state what the family rules are about going places and keeping safe, but this may be set aside at times (Moore 1986). A common justification used by children for ignoring parental injunctions is that this way they will learn for themselves (Lindon 1996).

It has been argued that adults have curtailed children's active participation in realms beyond home and school in recent decades, in part because of fears about safety and traffic (Ward 1994). Surveys of children aged seven to eleven in 1971 and 1990 showed a substantial reduction in the proportions who said they were allowed to walk to a park alone or take a bus ride unaccompanied by an adult (Hillman, Adams and Whitlegg 1990). This finding fits with the high levels of anxiety about abduction and traffic voiced by parents in our study.

Although children do not value formal parks and play areas, they are also attracted to 'wild' and 'secret' places, which they have more scope to make their own (Hart 1979; Naylor 1986). They like to create their own play environment, whether imaginatively or through using and moving materials provided by nature or left by adults. Favourite haunts may be given special names to heighten the sense of claiming space for their own uses (Matthews 1992).

Comforts and support

Most children's social networks expand during middle childhood, particularly through the addition of other children and non-related adults (Belle 1989; Cochran et al. 1990). However, the mere existence of social contacts does not guarantee the availability of trust and support. Having one or more people to discuss problems with is important to children and helps them cope with change and difficulties (Collings et al. 1995).

As in our studies, when children are asked to say who are the people most important to them or who provides support, they most often mention close relatives and friends, though a small number of non-related adults can also be significant to them (Belle 1989; Cochran et al. 1990; Savin-Williams and Berndt 1990). The largest numbers of children see their mothers as their main confidants (Ghate and Daniels 1997).

Up to about age eight, children usually see adults and especially parents as wholly or primarily responsible for their safety. Gradually thereafter, children accept a growing role for themselves in their own health and protection – and indeed help younger ones too (Williams et al. 1989; Mayall 1993).

Most primary-school teachers are well-liked by their pupils. The qualities which children appreciate most are – fairness, kindliness and a sense of humour (Cullingford 1991; A. Lewis 1995). However, Mayall (1994a) argues that children have much less ability to negotiate and alter rules and routines at school than they do at home.

Children and the media

Both parents and children in our studies identified the media, mainly television, as a significant influence on children's knowledge and attitudes. A survey of parental attitudes to health education identified television watching as significant concern of many parents. Some voiced worries that unregulated viewing encouraged such things as substance abuse, violence and early pregnancy (Balding 1988).

We do not need research to tell us that television and, increasingly, computers and videos are of great importance in the lives of many children. Adult anxieties about the possible or presumed disadvantages of spending much time watching television have meant that many studies have investigated the possible negative outcomes, with rather fewer examining possible benefits.

Both adults and children's programmes include a considerable amount of physical violence, much of which appears to cause little suffering (Gunter and Harrison 1997). Various reviews of the impact of violence on television have concluded that there is a modest link between exposure to this and actual aggressive behaviour. Correlations between type of viewing and aggressive acts may result as much from aggressive people seeking out violent programmes as the images causing the behaviour (Buckingham 1993; LeFrancois 1990). However, some research has shown an increase in conflict and restlessness among children exposed to an aggressive programme, compared with others who did not watch the same programme (Murray 1993).

There is also evidence that television can help children to be more altruistic and to make intellectual gains, though these benefits may be greater for children who were more advantaged in the first place (LeFrancois 1990; Murray 1993). Moreover, use of television is usually mediated by parents (Wober and Gunter 1988) and may be used by adult family members to reinforce cultural and religious identity (Gillespie 1993).

Adults also express concern that spending much time with television and computers is asocial or even anti-social. In fact, social engagement may be promoted. TV programmes and computer games have become a major topic of peer conversation, whilst network linkages can, like the telephone, enable children to communicate with others at a distance, even in other parts of the world (Buckingham 1994; Crook 1992). Children are not 'victims' of media influences, but are active and selective participants (Buckingham 1993).

Parents on parenting

Although it has been suggested that much more is known about parental viewpoints than those of children, much of this knowledge is based on personal and clinical experiences or observations. Surprisingly few systematic studies have taken account of parents' stated views, especially at this life stage. Academic texts which focus on parents and families tend to concentrate on observable behaviour and even then much more attention has been given to the pre-school years than the period covered by this book (see e.g. Dunn 1993; White and Woollett 1992).

Parents, mothers and fathers

How meaningful is it to talk about the common features of parents? Our sample of parents revealed a spectrum of opinion about the importance of parents' gender. Some regarded the expectations and responsibilities of mothers and fathers as radically different and also unequal. For others, the roles were seen as similar and overlapping.

The wider literature suggests that expectations and activities are sharply differentiated between mothers and fathers (Gittins 1993). In most families men have a secondary role in decision making and activities related to children's health and well-being (Brannen *et al.* 1994; Graham 1987; Hewison 1994; Mayall 1994b). Conventional ideologies transmitted at societal and biographical level have led most mothers to have a greater sense of investment in and personal responsibility for parenting than men (Kaplan 1992; Phoenix and Woollett 1991; Wetherell 1995). In the main, mothers are better informed about the details of their children's daily lives than are fathers (Hood *et al.* 1996). However patterns are highly variable and there have been some shifts towards greater involvement of men in child care over the last few decades (Moss 1996). On the other hand, there is much evidence that males and females can be equally competent and can carry out the same range of responsibilities, other than childbirth and breast-feeding (Schaffer 1990). Mothers with strong career commitments tend to believe that their psychological and social availability to their children is more important than physical omnipresence (Kaplan 1992).

Despite the widespread view that expectations about fatherhood have changed considerably since the 1950s, little systematic knowledge is available about how fathers themselves perceive their roles and much of the information about father–child interaction relates to pre-school children (Lamb 1987; C. Lewis 1995). A personal account by French (1995) voiced what appears to be a common tension between the wish that fathers be more participative and concerns that physical affection may be expressed or perceived as sexual abuse. Whilst some separated fathers are evidently harmful or indifferent towards the children and/or ex-partners, many find that sustaining contact with their children is hard. The reasons they give for this include practical difficulties, feelings of loss and guilt, and continuing tensions with the mother (Burgess 1997; Kruk 1993). On the other hand, divorced mothers have reported how much effort they often had to put into access arrangements. This involved much negotiation, organising and planning of activities for the weekend and holiday periods with the father. It could also require 'a lot of emotional work with children who might be reluctant to go or who may be difficult to settle on their return' (Smart 1997, pp.315–16).

Relatives and especially grandparents are often very involved in children's lives, taking on a number of roles including playmate, confidant or present-giver towards the child and offering support and alternative care to parents (Cochran *et al.* 1990; Smith 1991). Families of Asian origin tend particularly to spend much time together with the extended family (Campion 1995; Rashid 1996). A parent of South Asian background described such close integration:

> I believe in keeping ties within the family. We meet each other every two or three days. We shop together, go out together. Sleep over at each other's houses. We share almost every aspect of our lives together. (cited in Modood *et al.* 1994, p.24)

Parental goals

The parents of our study indicated that their main goals were to facilitate a gradual integration of their child into the world outside the family whilst protecting the child from external threats and social disapproval. These appear to be general aims amongst parents in Britain and elsewhere (Hallden 1991; Newson and Newson 1970b). Ensuring children's emotional and moral well-being is seen by many parents as their central task, laying the foundations for happiness in later life (Backett 1982). This strong future orientation has been described by Hallden as representing the 'child as project', which contrasts with the more present-directed perspectives of most children. Dahlberg (1996) suggests that some parents are particularly 'project-oriented', so that activities and decisions are directed by concerns about a child's perceived future needs. Encouraging learning is a central feature of this orientation. This is contrasted with a 'here and now orientation', when activities are valued for their own sakes and a child's development seen as evolving satisfactorily without too much conscious input.

For their children's general well-being, most parents recognise four related requisites (Stolz 1967; Hill 1987; Pugh *et al.* 1994):

- love and support to provide security
- guidance and control
- teaching and task allocation to develop responsibility for self and others
- encouragement and teaching to promote scholastic achievement.

Whilst there may be a fair amount of consensus at this global level, the detailed meaning and implementation of these values entails much more diversity of opinion, as does the management of their sometimes conflicting implications (e.g. between security and independence).

Most parents avow that their family commitments come first, though this principle usually has to be accommodated to two other important imperatives – first, sustaining a standard of living through work and, second, pursuing individualist goals (Jordan, Redley and James 1994). Managing these competing aims is generally much harder for women who often feel and are expected to have a greater responsibility to meet their children's needs than men (Segal 1995).

Autonomy and control

The balance of priorities alters gradually as children grow older. They typically spend increased amounts of time beyond the purview of parents or other adults. As a result, parents must guide their children's behaviour at a distance. Some form of 'co-regulation' becomes necessary (Collings *et al.* 1995, p.72), whereby parents teach, persuade or agree with their children how they should conduct themselves when they are apart. Several studies have shown how parents allow increased independence as children grow older (Kuczinski *et al.* 1987). It is recognised that keeping children home all the time may lead to social isolation, yet parents express concerns about physical and social threats like traffic, pollution and assault (Hood *et al.* 1996), as we too found.

Parents also tend to expect more and attribute more responsibility for misbehaviour, which may lead to conflict (Dix *et al.* 1989). By and large, both the demonstration of physical affection and the use of physical punishments decrease as children grow older (Collings *et al.* 1995; Newson and Newson 1976). Greater use is made of deprivation of privileges and verbal techniques designed to arouse or promote guilt and remind of rules. Many parents report that they are less strict and use physical punishment less in comparison with how they recall discipline in their own childhoods (Creighton and Russell 1996).

Several writers from Scandinavia have analysed parent–child negotiation of everyday life. Solberg (1990) learned from children aged around ten that they welcomed being home alone after school when their parents were working – a situation which resulted from negotiating with their parents not to spend time with after-school carers. Dahlberg (1996) concluded from her investigation that regular negotiation with children 'not only emphasises children's ability to plan and choose, but also their capacity to take and anticipate the consequences of their actions' (p.90). When considering parent–child interaction, a useful distinction may be made between decision making and activity. Based on interviews with nine- to thirteen-year-olds in lone-parent households, Alanen (1998) realised that some children's activities were largely integrated with their mothers', whereas others largely did separate things. However, organising those activities might be done jointly or singly in either case.

A study carried out in London suggested that between the ages of nine and twelve parents often expect their children to have more self-determination in the use of time, but growing consciousness about the importance of homework and of school achievement for future prospects fortifies a continued interest in intervening substantially in children's use of time (Hood *et al.* 1996). Parents also expected children to reconcile their own wishes with 'the interest of the family', which could mean countervailing adult wishes or the needs of siblings.

Early research identified class differences in parenting attitudes and styles, as well as considerable overlaps (Kohn 1969; Newson and Newson 1976). Working-class and middle-class parents apparently showed similar warmth and love towards their children and were equally concerned to promote their children's best interests but while middle-class children were encouraged to internalise values of achievement and responsibility, working-class parents were more concerned that their children should be obedient, conforming and respectable. Laybourn (1986) drew attention to the positive aspects of stricter working-class parenting styles, which helped protect young people from trouble with the law.

Cultural beliefs and practices can be very influential, though it is essential not to stereotype and over-generalise since each tradition encompasses variety. Parents of Indian and Pakistani backgrounds generally value considerable involvement of the extended family in decision making about children. Many expect their children to adhere closely to their parents' and elders' wishes. According to Dwivedi (1996), whereas Western cultures emphasise growth towards independence, 'the eastern cultures place more emphasis on "dependability"' (p.28) although the younger generation brought up in Britain often engage in more discussion with their children about the use of authority:

> There are a lot of things I accept that my parents would not accept – like my children telling me exactly what they think. (British parent of Caribbean background cited in Modood *et al.* 1994, p.18)

It is a commonplace of current sociological thinking that families are controlled in subtle ways by professionals like doctors, health visitors, teachers and social workers to serve the interests of the state (Jenks 1996; Parton 1991). The parents in our study and others tended to see the influences on their parenting as much more immediate – mainly their own upbringing and their current social networks, though some acknowledged the influence of their own work as professionals. Also some were very conscious of actual or potential professional 'surveillance' in relation to suspicions of child abuse or children's rights issues.

Parental concerns

A distinction may be made between daily concerns and fears about the unexpected. While many parents take for granted their children's physical well-being once they have survived infancy, for families and especially mothers living in poverty this often remains a constant worry (Middleton *et al.* 1995). There is much evidence that parents living in poverty make sacrifices to ensure that their children have adequate food and clothing (Dowler and Calvert 1995; Glendinning and Millar 1987). Poor parents often accede to their children's wishes to eat food which the parents think is not healthy because they cannot afford wastage of approved food which the child might not eat (Dobson, Beardsworth and Walker 1994).

One survey found, as we did, that the greatest fear of parents about their children was that they might be abducted (Kidscape 1993). The views of a large representative sample of parents were canvassed by questionnaires in 1997. The issues most frequently recorded as a concern were, in order:

- alcohol and drug abuse
- future employment or potential unemployment
- bullying
- lack of facilities
- children's materialism
- poor standards in schools.

In contrast to our study, no mention was made of concerns about the local neighbourhood. Three-quarters of parents also expressed support for changed working patterns so they can spend more time with their children, implicitly indicating agreement with children's views that parents are often not as available as they should be (NCH 1997).

Support for parents

A wide range of social and educational services are available to parents, though these are often poorly coordinated and irregular in their availability. Many are focused on the early years, when it is thought that pressures on parents are greatest and the scope for prevention of problems highest (Gibbons 1995; Roberts and MacDonald 1998). Help and guidance in middle childhood is less easy to come by. Support can be provided by professionals, through mutual support groups and by various kinds of written or visual media. Some provision is open to all, some is targeted at specific types of family or issue (Pugh *et al.* 1994). Approaches include behavioural, skill-based, relationship-oriented and community development (Smith 1997).

Conclusions

Theorising and research about children is shifting from an emphasis on apparent universal patterns and the identification of variations through statistical analysis to comprehending the diverse and socially created meanings of children's lives through more qualitative research. Middle childhood has been relatively neglected compared with the early years and adolescent.

In broad terms it appears that the findings of our two studies are consistent with evidence from other research. The core issues for children and parents during middle childhood entail managing and balancing a few key domains and relationships as shown in Figure 11.1:

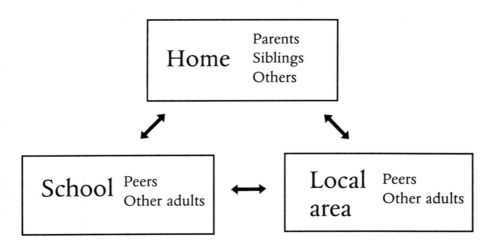

Figure 11.1: Key domains and relationships in middle childhood

Parents and friends are the prime sources of security, comfort and satisfaction, though also prominent causes of worries and unhappiness. Though many children have important relationships with kin living apart from them (including sometimes a separated parent), often family lives are focused on the household. Other children of the same age are very important in providing children with friendships, information and expectations. Many of children's worries centre on death, separation and loss within the extended family and on bullying and discrimination by peers.

During the primary-school years, children increasingly spend time moving about and playing in locations beyond home and school, either alone or with friends. Negotiation and rule-setting about children's independent action outside the home and responsibilities within the home is a major feature of parent–child communication. Whereas some parents appear to focus on their perceptions of children's current needs, others are very conscious of preparing their children's competencies for the future. Much of the responsibility for children's daily care and well-being rests with mothers much more than fathers.

The lives of parents and children, and the interactions between them, have been extensively documented. However, this has mainly been carried out by outsiders working to their own agendas and determining which aspects of family life merit attention. What is perhaps most striking is the dearth of studies which, like ours and a few others, seek the views of children and parents on issues which are of concern to them. As a result, we still know very little about the experience of middle childhood as seen through the eyes of its major participants.

CHAPTER 12

Rethinking Middle Childhood

A tale of two studies

We began this book by suggesting that the middle years of childhood are nowadays experienced by children, parents and others as subject to rapidly changing material, social and technological changes. It is also a period that has received little focused attention compared with the early years and the teen stage, which have both been viewed as involving much more turbulence, vulnerability and family tensions than middle childhood.

The picture which emerged from our two studies is more complex. It showed that many parents regarded this period as problematic. The children were on the whole less troubled, but drew attention to a number of their concerns to which they thought adults did not give sufficient attention. In the course of the book we have set alongside each other the views of children and parents on particular themes such as health, safety and rights. In this chapter, we shall summarise each of their perspectives separately and then draw out the main similarities and contrasts. Finally we note what may be some of the implications for families, professionals and policy makers.

Before doing so it is important to recall some of the strengths and weaknesses of the two studies on which this book has largely been based. They were carried out in a range of contrasting urban and rural areas in Central Scotland. Individual and group interviews were held with samples of children and parents, supplemented by brief self-completion questionnaires. Both were qualitative studies which aimed to ascertain the views of people themselves about what were the key issues for them. The first study set out to ascertain what children aged five to twelve regarded as the main elements in their emotional well-being and what the main influences on it were. This research involved over 100 children, of whom 69 were within the relevant age range considered in this book. The second study aimed to explore with a range of parents and a smaller number of children what they saw as the main issues with respect to parenting and health education in middle childhood. Seventy-five parents and 38 children took part. Contacts in both studies were virtually all one-off, so although many individuals seemed remarkably forthcoming, it is quite likely that certain deeper and more private issues were not revealed.

Both studies encouraged participants to set the agenda and to say what they saw as the most important issues affecting children's well-being and parenting. Hence we are reasonably confident that the research did tap into the main preoccupations of families with children in the middle age range. A school-based survey of somewhat older children reached broadly similar conclusions (Gordon and Grant 1996). Although the Parenting study inevitably focused on parent–child relationships, the family home was only one element of children's lives which featured in the two studies. They also showed the importance to children of their peer relationships, school and activities in the local neighbourhood and beyond.

The sampling processes and the need to obtain multiple agreements for participation probably mean that the adults and children we spoke with were not fully representative of the population at large. Certainly a good range of environments and of household structures were included. The social mix extended from well-off professional families to those struggling daily to make ends meet. However, some groups were not represented. Families making use of fee-paying schools were largely absent from the study, since recruitment was mainly through state schools. Children with significant communication or learning difficulties did not take part.

Other groups are likely to have been underrepresented. It seems probable that families going through major problems or who felt hostile to 'the authorities' would have been unlikely to participate, so that the study may paint an unduly positive view of family life. Although children from ethnic minority backgrounds were involved in the studies (almost all with parents of Pakistani, Chinese or Indian origins), numbers were relatively small (about 5%). It was therefore not possible to draw any general conclusions about the influences of racism and non-Western cultures, though this was clearly important for individual children. To represent their viewpoints it would be important to have more focused research, with opportunities to build up trust with adults from similar backgrounds (see e.g. Barn, Sinclair and Ferdinand 1997).

As a result of these sampling factors, the book has much to say about the experiences of a wide array of children and parents, but understanding of the detailed perspectives of certain minority groups and circumstances would require much larger scale or more specialist research. The main purpose of this chapter is to draw out general conclusions about matters which were common to most of the sample, so inevitably some of the variations and divergences will be underplayed.

The children's perspective

Happy and unhappy experiences

In general, the experience of middle childhood conveyed by the children themselves was of broad contentment and security, although mixed with a range of worries and fears. The exceptions were a few children whose lives had involved disruption and trauma.

Nearly all of the children seen individually said that they felt happy most days and that they experienced more negative feelings quite rarely. Most groups also chose 'happy' as one of three feelings that children experience often. Happiness usually arose from doing things with other people, especially friends. Some children also pointed to the significance of times when they felt important because of an individual or group achievement, like winning a competition. Feelings of safety on the other hand were mostly linked to the comforting presence of adults, usually parents, in situations of fear.

Children spoke of feeling worried, sad or fearful in a wide variety of situations. The most common were:

- falling out with friends
- being bullied or teased by peers
- being told off by parents
- adults breaking promises
- actual or potential separation of parents
- sibling disputes
- perceived favouritism or unfairness by teachers or parents
- death and illness of close relatives
- fears of what to most adults are imaginary things (like ghosts)
- situations of danger.

In the main, these were related to common, everyday happenings.

Children's key relationships

With a few important exceptions, the children's statements indicated that they mostly took for granted basic love and care within their own families. They also indicated a high degree of trust in adults more generally, as other studies have found (Moran *et al.* 1997). Their two main sources of support were parents and other children. The great majority in the sample expressed positive views about adults, with a high degree of confidence shown by the great majority in their parents. However, a number did point to what they felt as neglect by parents who were often busy or distracted. Not uncommonly, other relatives were also important confidants or playmates, but in only a few cases were people other than parents or friends cited as key helpers in a child's life. Nearly all the children had at least a few best friends they included in their charts of their most significant network members (ecomaps).

Teachers were generally trusted and well respected, but perhaps less prominent in the children's conversations than might have been expected. They will probably not be surprised to hear that they are expected to be as fair and impartial as possible.

Some parents and schools seemed, by their children's accounts, to be particularly good at giving them opportunities to achieve and at recognising important life events, thus contributing greatly to the children's sense of self-esteem. Children also stressed the importance of continuity. They expressed worries about parental tensions and were upset when friendships broke down.

Pets were important to many children, even some of the older ones. They were sometimes valued for their very lack of human qualities like breaching confidences or telling you off.

Children's views on helping responses

When children experienced sadness, worries and other negative feelings, they normally wanted a combination of sympathy and intervention, but in varying degrees, depending on the circumstances. Some distress was seen as part and parcel of everyday life, and consequently not as something to be avoided, but to be alleviated or to be left alone with. This could apply to something as serious as bereavement, as well as more minor upsets.

Probably the most common wish for adult intervention centred on situations which they perceived as unjust or where they felt harassed by someone else. The former included situations where they felt they were not listened to, not believed or falsely accused. The latter mostly concerned circumstances when they wanted peers or siblings reprimanded or chastised, but also occasions when they thought adults were treating themselves badly.

With regard to peer difficulties, the level of help they desired was related to the type of situation. At one extreme, children wanted strong and effective action taken with respect to 'bullies' and 'troublemakers'. At the other, they expected to be able to deal with minor tiffs themselves and sometimes thought that adults made things worse through acting without understanding the subtle dynamics in the relationships. In the middle were more serious friendship breakdowns. Here children did not usually want active intervention by adults, but they did want them to realise how distressed they felt and to show sympathetic support.

In general, the children had one or more people they said they would confide in about concerns or fears. In some situations, simply telling someone was seen as sufficient to ease the worry. Some stressed the importance of confidentiality. On the other hand, certain children made clear that they sometimes preferred to be left alone to get over a slight or upset in their own way and in private. At least up to ages nine to ten, children usually welcomed physical comfort, particularly from parents.

Comments indicated a dislike of not being believed or of having worries and fears belittled by parents or other adults. Children also resented adults giving false or glib reassurance and making assumptions about their needs. An important message to adults about helping children in distress is to discuss with the child his or her views about the best way to proceed.

Evidently children were a major positive resource to each other, as well as being at times the source of difficulties. Many of the children gave examples of circumstances where they wanted help from their peers or thought they could offer help themselves. Often their typical responses to a child who was worried or sad involved giving immediate advice or an instant offer to provide an alternative arrangement (e.g. play with me if you have no friends; stay with me if you are not happy at home). Some showed an ability to explore the causes of problems more fully, before reacting. In the parenting study, children described instances where they were active in helping and caring for parents.

When asked what would improve children's lives, some suggestions were to have more enjoyable food, activities and objects. However, especially from the older ones, the most common wish was for adults to give more genuine attention and respect to children. Simply having adults spend time with them was asked for by several. Other requests were to be listened to more, taken seriously and understood.

Issues which were not prominent concerns

There were some subjects prominent in political, professional and educational circles which were absent or muted in the children's descriptions of their worlds. It appears that when prompted children admit to major concerns about wars and disasters (Silverman *et al.* 1995), but these were barely mentioned by children we spoke to. Presumably this is because they are distant in time and place from such events, although they would be exposed to images in the media. They have fortunately been spared the experiences of children in war zones or even in parts of the United States where witnessing shootings and murder is a common event (Melton 1994). Most had not been exposed to the life-threatening hardship which is rife in some parts of the world, though some were living in very deprived circumstances by British standards.

The children did not express concerns about their health or accidents. The sampling process will probably have excluded children with major physical disabilities or who had recently had serious injuries. However, some children were upset by the illness and death of loved ones, notably grandparents.

There were only occasional and sometimes oblique references made to the dangers from strangers, which has figured prominently in the media and in school programmes during recent years (Gillham 1991). Only a few older children mentioned drugs or alcohol affecting family members or potentially themselves. The dangers of motor accidents were also conspicuous by their absence. Whilst a number of children expressed worries about separation and divorce, nobody mentioned issues to do with step-parenting.

It is interesting that in the main the children were not demanding greater freedoms. In terms of children's rights, only a few emphasised perceived defects in their rights to security, provision, protection and autonomy. What they chiefly stressed were their participatory rights. In other words, they wanted their wishes to be ascertained and taken account of.

Differences between children

As noted above, the studies were primarily intended to give voice to as wide as possible range of children's views. Many differences were detected, but no attempt was made to correlate these with children's characteristics in a systematic way.

Age differences were apparent. Compared with the five- and seven-year-olds who were in the Well-being study, though not described in this book, the older primary school children expressed more awareness of the wider world beyond home and school. Many still took pleasure in treats, pets and individual outings, but they also reported satisfactions and disappointments in relation to a wider range of people and collective events like football games and singing competitions. Few expressed strong misgivings about adults (they were after all being interviewed by adults!), but more older children did question adult rules and competence.

There was agreement amongst most of the children that girls and boys differ significantly in the ways they typically behave and express emotions. As other studies have found (e.g. Hartup 1996; McGurk 1992) more girls were concerned about intense friendships (and break-ups), whereas many boys spent more time in group activities like football, with their emotions more invested in success or failure than in intimate relationships. Many of the children had definite views about differences between boys and girls (e.g. girls are more expressive, boys fall out with friends less often).

Contrary to many adult ideals about the quiet safety of the countryside, children living in the rural areas evinced a wider range of anxieties and fears about their environment. This in part seemed to reflect the fact that they had more freedom to roam than their urban counterparts and so more often encountered alarming situations outside the home without a familiar adult at hand.

The parents' perspectives

The children were mainly asked for their views on what affected their well-being and health and on how other people (adults and children) could assist. The parents were invited to discuss these too, but were also asked more specifically about the role and needs of parents in promoting their children's well-being.

Parents were not specifically asked whether they thought their children were happy or not most of the time. It may be that many took this for granted. However, the predominant feeling conveyed by parents was that of anxiety about their children's safety and well-being. They stressed the difficulties of raising children in modern Britain. They worried about what they saw as external threats and pressures which were hard for them and their children to deal with.

Children's well-being

The central ingredients of children's well-being were seen by parents in very similar terms to those identified by psychologists (Pringle 1980; Pugh et al. 1993). These included feeling loved and secure, knowledge and employability, good physical health, self-confidence, competent self-care, social skills and respect for others. Encouragement and praise were seen as important needs of children too. Emphasis was placed on social acceptability and responsibility, so that a key parental task at this stage was to promote children's involvement in social and recreational activities.

Many parents apparently assumed that their children's physical needs were amply met. Those on low incomes, however, stressed the difficulties of providing adequate food and clothing. They described careful strategies and self-sacrifices they used to try to ensure that their children were adequately fed. Nearly all parents were aware of what a 'healthy' diet for their children should consist of, but poor parents could not always afford the luxury of buying vegetables and fruit which were expensive or might not be eaten (see Ward 1995).

The need for safety figured very prominently in parents' discussions. Parents from a wide variety of urban and rural environments all expressed fears about social and physical dangers in the vicinity as a major threat to their children's well-being. The main hazards they spoke of were abduction, abuse, harassment, bullying, traffic and enticement by peers into crime or drug-taking.

Most parents stressed that children should be listened to and communicated with openly. Many regarded physical comfort at still very important at this age. Parenting was depicted as a reciprocal process in which parents responded to the variations in perceived, felt and expressed needs of children as individuals.

The role of parents and others in caring for and helping children

Parents' perceptions of their roles were implicitly located within a lifespan perspective. They recognised that children aged eight to twelve want and are capable of much greater mobility and independence than when younger. Already they thought very much in terms of preparing their children for adulthood. Conscious of a competitive employment environment and of various health and lifestyle risks, most saw a strong need to promote their children's education and to protect them from social hazards they were expected to encounter once in secondary school.

Parents varied in the extent to which they recognised their children's competence and this usually corresponded with status and power differentials. Most parents expected that their greater life experience and their supply and control of money put them in a better position to decide on what was best for a child and, if need be, ensure that happened. Some, however, did see their children as having equal or even superior understanding in some respects, especially in the management of their own separate spheres of activity, as at school, in organised activities or local play.

To varying degrees parents recognised the importance of negotiating with their children at this age about how they spent their time, where they went, with whom and at what times. Some believed that children were best protected by firmly applied rules, whilst others put more faith in encouraging children to learn how to be responsible and move about safety. The main disciplinary mechanisms used were apparently verbal admonishments and deprivation of privileges. Smacking was seen as a legitimate last resort, though its decreasing impact and hence use as children grew older was generally acknowledged. Some hard-pressed parents, especially in inner-city areas, felt at a loss to know how to control (and protect) their children as they wished.

As a result of their multiple concerns, most parents curtailed children's opportunities for independent travel and play outdoors more than they recalled happening to themselves when young. This was linked to a perception that the life outside the home has become more dominated by traffic and violence. Less attention was given to preparing children to protect themselves from adults known to them, although abuse by familiar people is encountered by a significant minority of children (Gillham 1991, 1994).

Although parents recognised that it was important for their children to be socially accepted amongst their age-mates, they tended to perceive peer influences as largely negative. In their eyes, it was peers who created excessive material expectations and encouraged anti-social activities. Children's demands for fashionable clothes and trainers were experienced as stressful by parents, particularly those on low incomes. Such requests were thought to be prompted by peer pressure and television advertising.

Children's rights

This disquiet about the demands made by their own children in the context of peer and media pressures coloured parents perceptions of children's rights. Nearly all parents had a narrow conception of these. They thought that the movement to extend children's rights mainly involved strengthening children's ability to disregard what parents and other adults want. Thus their awareness of the 'rights' discourse was limited to participatory rights (i.e. children's entitlement to have their say and influence decisions affecting them) and did not include rights to health, development, protection or services. Moreover, parents' ideas about participatory rights mainly embodied concerns that the law and rights activists increasingly support children being able to *determine* what happens, when in fact the main thrust has been to ensure that children's views are *taken into account* (Marshall 1997). As a result of this partial understanding, parents tended to view a framework of formal rights as worrying, threatening and undermining. Yet in their descriptions of everyday life, it was clear that parents did accept that children have certain moral rights to protection and participation. They were at pains to respond to what they saw as children's needs for love, safety and so on. Many also referred to giving children choices and opportunities to contribute their views. This was done within limits, though. It was the parents who determined the spheres where negotiation was allowed and who set boundaries round children's influences on rules and decisions. In the main, they expected to be in control.

Mothers and fathers

Opinion was sharply differentiated on the importance of parents' gender. Views were not simply divided along male–female lines, although more women recognised that they tended to have wider and greater responsibilities towards children than men, as all the academic evidence reviewed in the previous chapter suggests. Some noted sharp differences in both role expectations and performance by men and women. This perspective was prominent among the lone mothers, but not confined to them. An alternative view was that the functions of mothers and fathers at this stage are shared and interchangeable. This opinion was voiced more often by men, but also by some women.

Overall orientation to middle childhood

Several interconnected themes were evident in most parents' conversations. These may be summarised as follows:

Adolescence arrives early. The way many parents depicted middle childhood resembled more the stereotypical view of adolescence than the quiet, pragmatic period of developmental psychology texts (Bee 1995; LeFrancois, 1990). For example parents referred to puberty in girls from as young as eight years; they characterised many children as posing challenges to parental authority in various ways, and they talked about the strong and negative influence of peers. Also parents were very conscious of preparing children for adult life – this was a justification for many of their actions and rules.

Middle childhood thus appears to be a period of *worry and stress* for parents. Threading through parental accounts of specific issues was an overarching anxiety for and about their children. This was related to an image of children as growing in confidence and competence, yet remaining vulnerable and inexperienced.

The family and home were seen as a *haven in a threatening world* (see Lasch 1977). Parents were very aware that their children increasingly spent time in activities outside home and school and often wanted to spend more time without adult supervision. Yet parents mostly saw the realm beyond their direct influence as threatening. First, it presented dangers for children, as noted above. Second, social and professional attitudes were seen to undermine parents (e.g. by conferring more rights on children, by high levels of suspicion about physical contact and chastisement). Television and newspapers were seen as ambiguous – located in the home, yet powerful media of external influence.

As a result of these perceptions, the core process in relationships with the children was one of *negotiating a balance between parental control and children's autonomy* as to how and where children spent their time (and to some extent their money). 'Control' was the word used by the parents, who portrayed this mainly in terms of protecting children. Parents differed in the extent to which they wished or felt able to impose restrictions on children (for their own welfare, in parental eyes) or sought to negotiate agreed rules and arrangements with their children.

The local neighbourhood is the critical locus for parenting at this stage. Variations in experience were crucially affected by the social, structural and environmental differences which made up the local context for the movement and activities of children. In general, parental worries in the inner-city area were more immediately related to direct experience of problems than in the other areas. However, discussion of children's permitted 'territorial range' – i.e. how far and when they were allowed to travel alone, with siblings or with friends – figured prominently in parental discussions in all areas.

Children's and parents' views compared

It should be remembered that the two studies were not set up to compare directly the perspectives of adults and children. They were asked to discuss distinct, though overlapping, sets of questions and topics. Moreover, we did not obtain the views of parents and children within the same family. Nevertheless, the samples came for a similar spread of areas and backgrounds. Other research has supported certain of the main findings, as we saw in the last chapter. In consequence, it seems legitimate to compare cautiously the issues and concerns raised by the separate samples of children and parents.

In general the children's perspectives were mainly focused on their current lives and immediate experiences. Both their joys and their anxieties were linked to present or recent experiences, though some of the older ones did voice concerns or ambitions about academic and employment careers. In contrast, parents appeared more preoccupied with future and long-term issues, though this may have been partly prompted by the nature of the questions linked to the overall goals and needs of parents. The adults also expressed much more anxiety about threats to their children's well-being from the local neighbourhood and from wider social forces.

Correspondingly, the children thought that adults tended to underestimate the importance of their immediate anxieties and distress. They themselves seemed less bothered than the parents about dangers that as yet were on the margins of their temporal and spatial horizons, such as drugs or violence by strangers.

Children and parents were in agreement with each other and with the literature on the main needs of children and hence the corresponding tasks of parents. These centred on physical care and protection; love and affection; listening and attention; and preparation for adult life. Seemingly humdrum activities like providing meals were significant signs to children that they were really cared for.

Parents' perceptions of their children included a complex mix. They were regarded as competent in many ways yet as still lacking certain understandings of risk; they could move and act independently, but still required parents to do many things for them; they were vulnerable, though more able to avoid harm than when younger; they had elements of innocence, but were exposed to knowledge from peers and the media which parents disapproved of but often felt powerless to control. Although some analysts have sought to characterise whole historical epochs in terms of a primary orientation towards children as innocent, evil, vulnerable, playful or whatever (Hendrick 1990; Jenks 1996), doubtless adult attitudes have always been complicated and varied. Parents had strong images of their children as vulnerable and potentially corrupt, both of which gave rise to a perceived need for close supervision. Only a minority sought to impose total control, however. The majority said they tried to blend guidance and limit-setting with some degree of freedom which acknowledged the children' capabilities and responsibilities.

In several respects, the children also depicted their lives as a blend of dependence and independence. Family and especially parents were still vitally important for their sense of overall security and for turning to in times of difficulty or crisis. However, the children also made clear how central to them were relationships and activities with their friends and peers, who were responsible for many of the highs and lows of their lives. Children's positive roles towards each other as helpers, confidants and so on was not much acknowledged by parents, who tended to depict peers either neutrally as playmates and companions or else negatively as influencing their own children to deviate from and ignore parental wishes.

Both parents and children felt that it was important for communication between them to be two-way and both expected that the final say on most matters would rest with parents. Where they differed more was in their perceptions of what happened in practice. Although children did usually appreciate the love, help and support received from parents, many also registered the fact that parents were less available for them than they would have wanted. This could mean not being around when wanted or not tuning in to the child's feelings, so that both their satisfactions and worries were thought to be undervalued.

It also seemed that children voiced and described more caring attitudes and activities towards their parents than parents themselves acknowledged. Many of the children saw their parents as stressed; just as the adults themselves did. This invoked in many children gratitude that they themselves were largely preserved from worries about money and work, though some wanted to share and help with such anxieties. A widespread wish was for parents and adults to be less busy, so they could attend more fully to their children's feelings and wishes.

Despite their often vehement opposition to the abstract idea of children's rights, nearly all the parents indicated that negotiation was a key feature of this stage, unlike early childhood when parents are much more likely to plan for and insist on what their children eat, wear and do. Children of eight years and over were seen as often able to argue their own case and act responsibly. Surprisingly perhaps, few children complained that they wanted much more say in their lives. Possibly their parents did by and large involve them adequately in decisions. Possibly the children had low expectations about how much influence they could or should have.

Comments on situations of parental separation and divorce figured in both studies, though only in the Parenting study was it a specific object of questioning. The main specific references by children were to the sense of divided loyalties which are commonly though not invariably experienced in these circumstances (Parkinson 1987). A more pervasive effect of the wide-spread breakdown of partnerships is that many children in two-parent households can be sensitised to rows and are afraid that these foreshadow the break-up of the family. Parents generally acknowledged the importance of children maintaining contact with a separated parent, but also stressed that the responsibility for regulating this and other aspects of the child's life should be vested mainly in the parent who was looking after the child on a daily basis. Not having a say about the nature of visiting arrangement could then be a source of distress or resentment for the child.

One of the main divergences between parents and children's views was evident in the kinds of things they said they were most worried about. The children's worries and fears were mainly related to their immediate personal relationships. Most common were rows with friends, bullying and taunting by peers, unfair punishments or broken promises (usually by parents) and anxieties about family breakdown. There was little mention of the issues which were at the forefront of parents' minds and which are also for the most part central to media concerns and social education. Issues like drugs, sex and crime seemed close and threatening to parents, but were near or beyond the distant geo-graphical or time horizons of most children.

Many parents felt both ignorant and alarmed about illegal drugs, but few children mentioned these. Older children were aware of the dangers of drugs in the abstract, but the reality apparently seldom impinged on their lives. The evidence from other research is that this situation changes rapidly once children go to secondary school, by when exposure to illegal drug-taking, mainly cannabis, becomes widespread (Barnard, Forsyth and McKeganey 1996). Both adults and children seemed relatively nonchalant about alcohol, even though excessive consumption of this devastates the lives of many individuals and families. Children often expressed great disapproval of smoking cigarettes, including sometimes by their own parents, while a good many parents accepted smoking by children as inevitable. Sex did not appear to be a major interest for the children (although they may have been too embarrassed to mention this). It was a major concern of parents, usually discussed alongside worries about HIV and Aids.

Desired changes

In each study, children and parents were asked what they thought should be done, either to improve children's well-being or to support parents who have children in mid-childhood.

What children suggested

In the Well-being study children were invited at the end of each group or individual interview to compile a written list of suggestions of what grown-ups could do to 'help children have happy feelings more of the time'. Interestingly, although we did not specify which adults we were referring to, most children seemed to think in terms of their parents, reflecting the central role of parenting in the promotion of well-being.

This exercise produced a wide range of suggestions, but the most common things the children said they wanted from adults can be grouped as below. They are listed in the rough order of the frequency with which they occurred. The examples are for the most part in the children's own words as recorded on flip-charts:

- *Attention*: spend more time with them, play with them, take them places, don't leave alone in the house, make time to do things with them even on weekdays, give more attention in spare time.

- *Understanding*: listen to their problems, pay more attention, be more sensitive, remember what it is like to be a child, realise what life is like today, take children's concerns seriously, understand, remember children have feelings too.

- *Openness*: don't talk behind their back, talk to them, explain things to them, e.g. marital problems.

- *Treats*: buy them things, cook what they want, take them on holidays.

- *Freedom*: don't interfere with their lives and friendships, let them go to the park, let them make important decisions.

- *Non-indulgence*: don't spoil, don't give too many toys, be more strict.

- *Comfort*: reassure if worried, reassure them.

- *Encouragement*: help them be confident; encourage them.

- *Improved adult behaviour*: stop smoking, drinking and swearing, don't be moody.

Many more of the older children urged greater attention and understanding, whereas pleas for treats were more common among the younger children.

Especially by the age of eleven, but also often before that, children were asking to be taken more seriously. They wanted more time, genuine attention and empathy. More explaining was required – whether of adult problems or of expectations about children's behaviour. A further wish was for their own growing maturity to be recognised through allowing them to make some decisions and handle some situations themselves.

Several of the groups were fired with enthusiasm at the idea of a booklet for parents, which was subsequently produced, based on their sayings and drawings (HEBS 1997). One group of nine-year-olds children came up with a particularly snappy idea for the booklet to encapsulate their main message:

- *STOP* – and think about children's point of view

- *LOOK* – for their feelings

- *LISTEN* – to what they say.

'Stop, look and listen' is, of course, the catch phrase for a road safety campaign for younger children. It was a neat twist to turn this into a 'Highway Code' of parenting.

Somewhat fewer ideas were put forward about how children could help each other more. They mentioned sharing, explaining, including and supp-orting. Friendship was again prominent, with an emphasis on helping to ensure that nobody was left out of friendship networks. Avoidance of bullying and picking on others was also thought to be important. Clearly, children can make a significant contribution to each others' well-being, and have the motivation to do so.

What parents suggested

Since the parenting study was funded by a health education body, it included questions about areas in which parents thought they needed information and advice. As we noted in Chapter 10, the topics on which people thought information would be helpful included:

- illegal drugs, smoking, alcohol
- puberty, telling children about sex, HIV and Aids
- homosexuality
- empowering children to resist abusive behaviour
- controlling unruly children
- impact of adolescence
- how to listen to children
- children's needs for care and attention
- children's rights
- racism
- availability of local services e.g. psychological services, drug advice.

Easily the most frequent request was for information on drugs; nearly all the parents realised that there were big gaps in their knowledge in this area. This contributed to their sense of inadequacy and powerlessness when discussing the issue with their children. Information on the emotional and physical aspects of puberty was also requested. When it came to sex education, though, parents not only wanted information but advice on how to impart this to their children. Many admitted to difficulty in talking to their children about sex.

A number of parents thought that others would benefit from some education on children's needs for care and attention, how to listen to them and how to respect their rights. Those with children they found unruly wanted advice on how to handle their children and gain better cooperation. A few people thought that a directory of local services would be helpful.

In addition to suggesting what topics would helpful, parents gave some useful suggestions about the methods which would effectively get the information across. Many people recognised that the messages were complex and that it would be difficult to present them in such a way that they would be accessible to a wide range of parents. Some people suggested that since communication between parents and children was the key issue, a booklet or other medium should be prepared which was aimed at both and could be looked at together. Other ideas also incorporated the notion that guidance material should convey similar messages to both parents and children, fostering discussion between them, rather than be designed and delivered to each separately.

When people thought of health education they initially thought of posters, adverts on television and written material. Posters were dismissed as unsuitable for conveying complex messages. Television was recognised as a powerful influence on children and useful source of information. Several parents suggested this medium could be used more effectively. The implication was that health education should be directed at television, advertising and commercial companies. Documentaries and appropriate use of story lines on children's TV were suggested.

A number of people said a leaflet would be helpful. It was emphasised that this should be distributed widely, through schools or in places where people congregate, for example doctor's surgeries or social work offices. Other parents dismissed the idea of leaflets on the grounds that they can convey only superficial points and people are bombarded by literature so pay minimal attention to them. Several thought that a book covering a range of topics in some detail would be appropriate. It was observed that plenty of books cover preparation for parenthood and the early years, but then the supply of guidance dries up.

Many parents thought that schools played a less vital role in health education than they should. There were some complaints that parents knew very little of what was being taught. It was proposed that school materials on health-related issues be shared with parents as well as children. There were also suggestions of ways in which schools could modify their non-curricular activities to encourage health education messages to be put into practice. For example they could offer more imaginative PE classes, sell sugar-free drinks at lunchtime, provide wholesome food and introduce rewards for children who chose to eat in a healthy way. There was a widely held view that integrating health education into everyday life in this way would be more effective than traditional teaching methods. A further important message was that teachers often appeared to tell parents what to do and to direct teacher–parent communications, instead of acting in a more collaborative way so that parents could help shape the nature of their involvement with schools.

Other ideas involved provision of supportive services. In acknowledging how difficult this life stage could be for parents, there were some requests for an informal, non-stigmatised service where parents could get advice or talk over problems which were worrying them but did not yet need the full attention of a professional. Others wanted ready access to expert advice for specific problems. Many valued the opportunity to talk with other parents who had

had similar problems. One suggestion which combined elements of both mutual support and professional help was to have workshops on specific topics, such as puberty. Again the suggestion was that they should be arranged through schools. Some people liked the idea of a helpline for parents, though again there were different views about whether an expert or an experienced parent should be at the other end of the line.

Many parents pointed out that measures other than education were needed to improve parenting and children's well-being. Some parents thought that more than enough advice was available and what was needed was practical support services. Providing activities for children, increasing families' income or improving school or health services would have more of an impact. Environmental and social action was needed to combat pollution, drug-taking or solvent abuse.

Implications

In this book we have sought to bring together the opinions and experiences of a wide range of parents and children on what they see as the main issues which arise in middle childhood. This is the stage when in modern Britain children are in the second half of primary school. They have yet to reach adolescence and secondary school, which respectively have been seen as the main stepping stones to adult knowledge, employment, sexual activity, autonomy and responsibility. Research suggests that for most young people, the teen years are traversed with much less stress, discontinuity and alienation from adults than is popularly believed (Coleman and Hendry 1990; Noller and Callan 1991; Roche and Tucker 1997).

The studies summarised in this chapter, and supported by the literature reviewed in the previous chapter, suggest that middle childhood is also somewhat different from the conventional image. For parents it often entails intense anxieties, dilemmas about control and freedom, and awareness of future prospects and hazards. Perhaps a mark of the success of parents, teachers and others is that most children appear to be quite happy for most of the time. Alongside family involvement, they are closely immersed in a world of peers and media influences which they mostly enjoy, but which entail potential tensions between home and the outside world (see also Collings *et al.* 1995).

The studies also emphasised that this stage of middle childhood (in modern UK settings) does involve certain common themes such as the negotiation of freedom and boundaries as regards children's increasing independent mobility and intellectual skills. On the other hand, many features of middle childhood are very specific to the particular child, family and neighbourhood. Parents were very much aware that key features of family life had changed dramatically since they were young. As many sociologists and some psychologists are now stressing, the nature and meaning of childhood experiences and development are a product of complex and active interactions within specific material, historical and social contexts (James and Prout 1997; Sommer 1998).

Implications for families

Parents and children both acknowledge that dialogue is a vital ingredient in managing the transition between early childhood dependence and the relative autonomy of adolescence and adulthood. Yet our studies revealed a partial mismatch in perceptions and expectations. With some important exceptions, major conflicts were not present, but many parents were concerned about matters which were on the whole marginal to children, whilst many of the children felt adults should give them more time, understanding, recognition and open communication.

By and large, the study has not revealed wishes or needs for adults to *do* new things, but rather to attend more to children, in several respects. They should be around more of the time, listen more closely to what children say, and attend to their concerns. They must also pay heed to the great significance for children of events which adults may perceive as minor, trivial or even unreal. A small number of children who are unhappy or ill-treated would clearly like altered behaviour from adults, but for the rest a changed attitude is the main thing wanted, namely a willingness to listen and understand. This should of itself lead on to adults being more responsive to children in myriad detailed ways. It is also important for parents to recognise that children are valuable resources to each other, as well as sometimes causes of distress.

Implications for professionals and policy makers

Whilst we have largely concentrated on general features of family life at this stage, it is important to emphasise the importance of material and environmental contexts, whose uneven qualities impinge greatly on parents and children (see e.g. Townsend, Davidson and Whitehead 1982). Low income reduced options for healthy eating and opportunities for sport and family outings. Far too many children continue to be brought up in poverty, with major effects on their life chances. National policies and locally based initiatives are needed to address poverty for families, whether they have access to work and earned income or depend on benefits (Kumar 1993; Long 1995).

As our studies illustrated, families on the lowest incomes also often have to contend with local environments which are physically or socially more hazardous for children. Parents in city schemes were exposed to more stress and health risks than people living in the rural or suburban areas and had fewer resources to overcome them. Safety was a major issue in that real rather than potential dangers had to be confronted. Children talked about watching drug-users injecting and about the risks they posed in the area. Policy and community development measures can make an impact on such neighbourhoods (Cannan and Warren 1997; Roberts *et al.* 1995).

The predominant message from the children to all adults was to listen and take more seriously what children have to say. For the most part they were not seeking major changes in adult's behaviour, but they did want a new attitude which respected their viewpoints. This is consistent with the aspirations of the 'children's rights' movement, but our conversations with parents indicated a need for more dialogue and discussion about what children's rights involves, so that the key people in children's lives are not alienated and undermined. The children were also clear that they wanted adult intervention to deal more effectively with bullying, harassment and discrimination, both at school and in the local neighbourhood. It was important that they should be consulted about the precise ways in which adults should help. They were all too conscious of times when adults misconstrued situations and so made them worse rather than better. Before acting, adults should assess children's understandings of conflict or distress and check with them how this might best be dealt with.

Thus children did not see their rights to nurturance, protection and participation as in separate compartments. If adults listened and consulted more, this would enable them to be more sensitive about when and how to act to help children – or when it was best to leave children to sort things out themselves.

Many of the parents we spoke to felt they would benefit from information, advice or support. Yet as our discussion groups illustrated, this is not simply a matter of providing facts, important though that may be for some subjects such as drugs and HIV. Parents want and need to explore the significance of knowledge and values about children, so that this can be reconciled and integrated with their own experiences and viewpoints. At present some feel undermined by notions of children's rights (filtered by representations in the media and through their social networks) and by scrutiny in relation to child abuse.

Dialogue is needed between professional and lay ideas about rights and risk. Parents are highly concerned about safety and adopt strategies to protect children outwith the home. Relatively little attention is paid to preparing children to protect themselves from people known to them, which the work of ChildLine and other agencies has shown is a significant risk. Parents' attempts to counter what they see as undesirable peer influences are likely to backfire if they ignore the crucial importance to children of their friendships and of wider social acceptability and are unaware of the subtle processes of interaction which expose them to drugs, bullying and so on.

At present, children and parents appear to be 'targeted' separately as regards such matters as sex education, drugs and smoking. It would be helpful to make available resources which encourage both groups to engage in joint activities. These might include a work book, video or computer package which parents and children could look at together and discuss.

Although schools sometimes find it hard to increase parental involvement, the parents in our study expressed a willingness to cooperate more closely with schools. It would help parents to know more details about the contents of personal and social education. Similarly, communication between parents and schools should involve more sharing of aims, ideas and materials in relation to health and social education. At present, it seems that many parents experience their involvement in schools, even though often quite positive, as a 'top-down' process rather than a genuine partnership.

Both the children and the parents in our studies seemed to appreciate the opportunity to come together to discuss everyday issues affecting them. The children valued the adult attention focused on themselves and enjoyed the interchanges with each other. Parents welcomed the chance to explore different perspectives and at times gain insights from what others said. This is a mechanism for education and support which is not widely available, but would be well received.

Concluding remarks

Middle childhood is a period when children and the other key players in their lives negotiate an increasingly complex and fast-changing world. It is a time of preparation for later life in economic, technological and environmental circumstances which are hard to predict, but it is also a time to be cherished for its own sake. With the marked physical dependency of early childhood over and the transitions to economic and other forms of autonomy still some way off, it is a time when children, parents and others have to manage a range of tensions and competing principles. Increasing freedom, exploration and responsibility are to be encouraged, whilst some form of protection is required as regards risks to health, well-being and moral or legal behaviour.

This book has conveyed a number of specific messages about children's and parents' perspectives on these issues in middle childhood. At its heart has been the theme of communication. Our writing has only been possible because people were willing to convey to us their views and concerns, which they knew would be passed on in various ways to policy makers, educators, professionals and the public. Possibly the most important conclusion to be drawn is that processes of dialogue are essential if more specific goals are to be achieved. Guidance to parents needs to connect with their concerns and views of the world. Guidance by parents and other adults to children needs to be informed by and take account of children's own wishes and understandings. The enjoyment, energy and commitment which both children and parents showed in discussions with us is a good omen.

References

Adams, R. (1995) 'Places of childhood.' In P. Henderson (ed) *Children and Communities*. London: Pluto Press.

Adler, P.A. and Adler, P. (eds) (1986) *Sociological Studies of Child Development*. Greenwich CT: JAI Press.

Alanen, L. (1997) 'Children and the family order: constraints and competencies.' In I. Hutchby and J. Moran-Ellis (eds.) *Children and Social Competences*. London: Farmer Press.

Alcock, P. (1993) *Understanding Poverty*. London: Macmillan.

Aldgate, J. (1988) 'Work with children experiencing separation and loss: a theoretical framework.' In J. Aldgate and J. Simmonds (eds) *Direct Work with Children*. London: Batsford.

Aldridge, J. and Becker, S. (1995) 'The rights and wrongs of children who care.' In B. Franklin (ed) *The Handbook of Children's Rights*. London: Routledge.

Amato, P.R. and Keith, B. (1991) 'Parental divorce and well-being of children: a meta-analysis.' *Psychological Bulletin 110*, 1, 26–46.

Archer, C. (1996) 'Attachment disordered children.' In R. Phillips and E. McWilliam (eds) *After Adoption*. London: BAAF.

Archer, J. (1992) 'Childhood gender roles: social context and organisation.' In H. McGurk (ed) *Childhood Social Development*. Hove: Lawrence Erlbaum.

Ariès, P. (1971) *Histoires des Populations Francaises*. Paris: Editions du Seuil.

Asher, S.R. and Coie, J.D. (eds) (1991) *Peer Rejection in Childhood*. Cambridge: Cambridge University Press.

Asquith, S. and Hill, M. (eds) (1994) *Justice for Children*. Dordrecht: Martinus Nijhoff.

Backett, K.C. (1982) *Mothers and Fathers*. London: Macmillan.

Backett, K.C. (1992) 'Taboos and excesses: lay health moralities in middle class families.' *Sociology of Health and Illness 14*, 2, 255–73.

Balding, J. (1988) *Parents and Health Education*. London: HEA.

Barn, R., Sinclair, R. and Ferdinand, D. (1997) *Acting on Principle*. London: BAAF.

Barnard, M., Forsyth, A. and McKeganey, N. (1996) 'Levels of drug use among a sample of Scottish schoolchildren.' *Drugs: Education, Prevention and Policy 3*, 1, 81–9.

Bee, H. (1989) *The Developing Child* (5th edition). New York: Harper Collins.

Bee, H. (1995) *The Developing Child* (7th edition). New York: Harper Collins.

Bell, R.Q. (1970) 'A reinterpretation of the direction of effects in studies of child socialisation.' In K. Danziger (ed) *Socialisation*. Harmondsworth: Penguin.

Belle, D. (1989) *Children's Social Networks and Social Supports*. New York: John Wiley.

Berg, M. and Medrich, E.A. (1980) 'Children in four neighbourhoods.' *Environment and Behaviour 12*, 3, 320–48.

Berndt, T.J. (1986) 'Children's comments about their friendships.' In M. Perlmutter (ed) *Cognitive Perspectives on Children's Social and Behavioural Development*. Hillsdale, NJ: Lawrence Erlbaum.

Berti, A.E. and Bombi, A.S. (1988) *The Child's Construction of Economics*. Cambridge: Cambridge University Press.

Bigelow, B.J., Tesson, G. and Lewko, J.H. (1996) *Learning the Rules*. New York: Guilford Press.

Blatchford, P., Creeser, R. and Mooney, A. (1991) 'Playground games and playtime: the children's view.' In M. Woodhead, P. Light and R. Carr (eds) *Growing Up in a Changing Society*. London: Routledge.

Bluebond-Langner, M., Perkel, D., Goertzel, T., Nelson, K. and Geary, J. (1990) 'Children's knowledge of cancer and its treatment: impact of an oncology camp experience.' *Journal of Pediatrics 116*, 2, 207–13.

Borland, M., Brown, J. Hill, M. and Buist, M. (1996) 'Parenting in Middle Childhood.' Report to the Health Education Board for Scotland, Edinburgh.

Boulton, M. (1995) 'Patterns of bully/victim problems in mixed race groups of children.' *Social Development 4*, 3, 277–93.

Bowlby, J. (1969) *Attachment*. Harmondsworth: Penguin.

Boyden, J. (1997) 'Childhood and policy makers.' In A. James and A. Prout (eds) *Constructing and Reconstructing Childhood* (2nd edition). London: Falmer Press.

Brannen, J., Dodd, D., Oakley, A. and Storey, P. (1994) *Young People: Health and Family Life*. Buckingham: Open University Press.

Brannen, J. and O'Brien, M. (eds) (1996) *Children in Families*. London: Falmer Press.

Bronfenbrenner, U. (1979) *The Ecology of Human Development*. Cambridge, MA: Harvard University Press.

Bruner, J. (1990) *Acts of Meaning*. Cambridge, MA: Harvard University Press.

Buckingham, D. (ed) (1993) *Reading Audiences: Young People and the Media*. Manchester: Manchester University Press.

Buckingham, D. (1994) 'Television and the definition of childhood.' In B. Mayall (ed) *Children's Childhoods Observed and Experienced*. London: Falmer Press.

Burgess, A. (1997) *Fatherhood Reclaimed*. London: Vermillion.

Burgoyne, J. and Clark, D. (1984) *Making a Go of It: A Study of Step Families in Sheffield*. London: Routledge & Kegan Paul.

Burman, E. (1994) *Deconstructing Developmental Psychology*. London: Routledge.

Butler, I. and Williamson, H. (1994) *Children Speak: Children, Trauma and Social Work*. London: NSPCC/Longman.

Campion, M.J. (1995) *Who's Fit to be a Parent?* London: Routledge.

Cannan, C. and Warren, C. (eds) (1996) *Social Action with Children and Families*. London: Routledge.

Cochran, M., Larner, D., Riley, D., Gunnarson, L. and Henderson, C.R. (1990) *Extending Families: The Social Networks of Parents and their Children*. Cambridge: Cambridge University Press.

Coie, J.D. (1991) 'Towards a theory of peer rejection.' In S.R. Asher and J.D. Coie (eds) *Peer Rejection in Childhood*. Cambridge: Cambridge University Press.

Coleman, J.C. and Hendry, L. (1990) *The Nature of Adolescence*. London: Routledge.

Collings, W.A., Harris, M.L. and Susman, A. (1995) 'Parenting during middle childhood.' In M.H. Bornstein (ed) *Handbook of Parenting: Children and Parenting* vol. 1. Hillsdale, NJ: Lawrence Erlbaum.

Cox, M.V. (1980) *Are Young Children Egocentric?* London: Batsford.

Creighton, S. and Russell, N. (1996) *Voices from Childhood*. London: NSPCC.

Crook, C. (1992) 'Cultural artefacts in social development: the case of computers.' In H. McGurk (ed) *Childhood Social Development*. Hove: Lawrence Erlbaum.

Cullingford, C. (1991) *The Inner World of School*. London: Cassell.

Dahlberg, G. (1996) 'Negotiating modern childrearing and family life in Sweden.' In J. Brannen and R. Edwards (eds) *Perspectives on Parenting and Childhood: Looking Back and Moving Forward*. London: South Bank University.

Dallos, R. (1995) 'Constructing family life and family belief systems.' In J. Muncie *et al.* (eds) *Understanding the Family*. London: Sage.

Davis, A. (1995) 'The impact of transport on children's health and well-being.' Paper presented to the conference on *Government Policies and their Effects on Children*. Preston: University of Central Lancashire.

Department of Health (1995) *Child Protection: Messages from Research*. London: HMSO.

Devine, M. (1995) *Health Education: What Do Young People Want to Know*. Edinburgh: SCRE.

Dimmock, B. (1997/8) 'The contemporary stepfamily: making links with fostering and adoption.' *Adoption & Fostering 21*, 4, 49–56.

Dix, T., Ruble, D.N. and Zambarano, R.J. (1989) 'Mothers' implicit theories of discipline: child effects, parent effects and the attribution process,' *Child Development 60*, 1373–1391.

Dobson B. Beardsworth A. and Walker, R. (1994) *Diet, Choice and Poverty*. London: Family Policy Studies Centre.

Donaldson, M. (1978) *Children's Minds*. London: Fontana.

Dowler, C. and Calvert, C. (1995) *Nutrition and Diet in Lone Parent Families in London*. London: Family Policy Studies Centre.

Downie, R.S., Fyfe, C. and Tannahill, A. (1990) *Health Promotion: Models and Values*. Oxford: Oxford University Press.

du Bois-Reymond, M., Buchner, P. and Kruger, H-H. (1993) 'Modern family as everyday negotiation: continuities and discontinuities in parent–child relationships.' *Childhood 1*, 87–99.

Dunn, J. (1993) *Young Children's Close Relationships*. London: Sage.

Dunn, J. and Plomin, R. (1990) *Separate Lives*. New York: Basic Books.

Dwivedi, K.N. (1996) 'Race and the child's perspective.' In R. Davie, G. Upton and V. Varma (eds) *The Voice of the Child*. London: Falmer Press.

Dwivedi, K.N. (1996) 'Culture and personality.' In K.N. Dwivedi and V.P. Varma (1996) *Meeting the Needs of Ethnic Minority Children*. London: Falmer Press.

Ennew, J. (1994) 'Time for children or time for adults.' In J. Qvortrup, M. Bardy, G. Sgritta and H. Wintersberger (eds) *Childhood Matters*. Aldershot: Avebury.

Erikson, E.H. (1965) *Childhood and Society*. Harmondsworth: Pelican Books.

Erwin, P. (1992) *Friendship and Peer Relations in Children*. Chichester: Wiley.

Fahlberg, V. (1982) *Child Development*. London: BAAF.

Fossey, E. (1994) *Growing Up with Alcohol*. London: Routledge.

Franklin, B. (ed) (1995) *The Handbook of Children's Rights*. London: Routledge.

French, S. (1995) 'The fallen idol.' In P. Moss (ed) *Father Figures*. Edinburgh: HMSO.

Ganetz, H. (1995) 'The shop, the home and femininity as a masquerade.' In J. Fornäs and G. Bolin (eds) *Youth Culture in Late Modernity*. London: Sage.

Garbarino, J., Stott, F.M. and associates (1992) *What Children Can Tell Us*. San Francisco: Jossey-Bass.

Gardner, R.A. (1994) *Understanding Children*. London: Aronson.

Garmezy, N. and Rutter, M. (eds) (1983) *Stress, Coping and Development in Children*. New York: McGraw-Hill.

Ghate, D. and Daniels, A. (1997) *Talking about MY Generation*. London: NSPCC.

Gibbons, J. (1995) 'Family support in child protection.' In M. Hill, R. Hawthorne-Kirk and D. Part (eds) *Supporting Families*. Edinburgh: HMSO.

Gibbons, J., Gallacher, B., Bell, C. and Gordon, D. (1995) *Development after Physical Abuse in Early Childhood*. London: HMSO.

Gillespie, R. (1993) 'The Mahabharata: from Sanskrit to sacred soap.' In D. Buchingham (ed) *Young People and the Media*. Manchester: Manchester University Press.

Gillham, B. (1991) *The Facts About Child Sexual Abuse*. London: Cassell.

Gillham, B. (1994) *The Facts About Child Physical Abuse*. London: Cassell.

Gittins, D. (1993) *The Family in Question*. Basingstoke: Macmillan.

Gittins, D. (1998) *The Child in Question*. Basingstoke: Macmillan.

Glendinning, C. and Millar, J. (eds) (1987) *Women and Poverty in Britain*. Brighton: Wheatsheaf.

Gordon, G. and Grant, J. (1997) *How We Feel: an Insight into the Emotional World of Teenagers*. London: Jessica Kingsley Publishers.

Graham, H. (1987) 'Women's poverty and caring.' In C. Glendinning and J. Millar (eds) *Women and Poverty in Britain*. Brighton: Wheatsheaf.

Gunter, B. and Harrison, J. (1997) 'Violence in children's programmes on British television.' *Children & Society 11*, 3, 143–56.

Hallden, G. (1991) 'The child as project and the child as being: parents' ideas as frames of reference.' *Children & Society 5*, 4, 334–46.

Hardyment, C. (1983) *Dream Babies.* London: Jonathan Cape.

Harris, P.L. (1992) *Children and Emotion.* Oxford: Blackwell.

Harris, P.L. (1994) 'The child's understanding of emotion: developmental change and family environment.' *Journal of Child Psychology and Psychiatry 35*, 1, 3–20.

Hart, R. (1979) *Children's Experience of Place.* New York: Irvington.

Hartup, W.W. (1992) 'Friendships and their developmental significance.' In H. McGurk (ed) *Childhood Social Development.* Hove: Lawrence Erlbaum.

Hartup, W.W. (1996) 'The company they keep: friendships and their developmental significance.' *Child Development 67*, 1–13.

HEBS (Health Education Board for Scotland) (1997) *Messages from Children.* Edinburgh: HEBS.

Hendrick, H. (1990) 'Constructions and reconstructions of British childhood: an interpretative survey, 1800 to the present.' In A. James and A. Prout (eds) *Constructing and Reconstructing Childhood.* London: The Falmer Press.

Hill, M. (1987) *Sharing Child Care in Early Parenthood.* London: RKP.

Hill, M. (1991) 'Concepts of parenthood and their application to adoption.' *Adoption & Fostering 15*, 4, 16–23.

Hill, M. (1992) 'Children's role in the domestic economy.' *Journal of Consumer Studies and Home Economics 16*, 33–50.

Hill, M. and Aldgate, J. (eds) (1996) *Child Welfare Services.* London: Jessica Kingsley Publishers.

Hill, M. and Tisdall, K. (1997) *Children and Society.* Harlow: Longman.

Hill, M., Laybourn, A. and Borland, M. (1995) *Children's Well-Being.* Report to the Health Education Board for Scotland: University of Glasgow.

Hill, M., Laybourn, A. and Borland, M. (1996) 'Engaging with primary-aged children about their emotions and well-being: Methodological considerations.' *Children & Society 10*, 2, 129–44.

Hill, M., Laybourn, A., Borland, M. and Secker, J. (1996) 'Promoting mental and emotional well-being: the perspectives of younger children.' In D. Trent and C. Reed (eds) *Promotion of Mental Health* vol. 5. Aldershot: Avebury.

Hillman, M. (ed) (1993) *Children, Transport and the Quality of Life.* London: Policy Studies Institute.

Hillman, M., Adams, J. and Whitlegg, J. (1990) *One False Move ... A Study of Children's Independent Mobility.* London: Policy Studies Institute.

Hogan, D. (1998) 'Valuing the child in research: historical and current influences on research methodology with children.' Proceedings of the Conference *Qualitative Research with Children,* Trinity College, Dublin.

Hogg, C., Barker, R. and McGuire, C. (1996) *Health Promotion and the Family.* London: Health Education Authority.

Holmes, J. (1993) *John Bowlby and Attachment Theory.* London: Routledge.

Hood, S., Kelley, P. Mayall, B., Oakley, A. with Morrell, R. (1996) *Children, Parents and Risk.* London: Institute of Education.

Howe, D. (1995a) *Attachment Theory for Social Workers.* London: Macmillan.

Howe, D. (1995b) 'Adoption and attachment.' *Adoption & Fostering 19*, 4, 7–17.

Howe, D. (ed) (1996) *Attachment Theory and Child and Family Social Work.* Aldershot: Avebury.

Hutchby and J. Moran-Ellis (eds) (1998) *Children and Social Competence.* London: Falmer Press.

Ives, R. (1991) *Soluble Problems: Tackling Solvent Sniffing by Young People.* London: National Children's Bureau.

Jackson, S., Fischer, M. and Ward, H. (1995) 'Key concepts in looking after children: parenting, partnership and outcomes.' In S. Jackson and S. Kilroe (eds) *Looking After Children: Good Parenting, Good Outcomes.* London: The Stationery Office.

James, A. (1993) *Childhood Identities.* Edinburgh: Edinburgh University Press.

James, A. and Prout, A. (eds) (1990) *Constructing and Reconstructing Childhood: Contemporary Issues in the Sociological Study of Childhood.* London: Falmer Press.

James, A. and Prout, A. (1995) 'Strategies and structures: towards a new perspective on children's experiences of family life.' In J. Brannen and M. O'Brien (eds) *Children and Families.* London: Falmer Press.

James, A. and Prout, A. (eds) (2nd Edition) (1997) *Constructing and Reconstructing Childhood: Contemporary Issues in the Sociological Study of Childhood.* London: Falmer Press.

Jenks, C. (1996) *Childhood.* London: Routledge.

Jones, G. and Wallace, C. (1992) *Youth, Family and Citizenship.* Buckingham: Open University Press.

Jordan, B., Redley, M. and James, S. (1994) *Putting the Family First.* London: UCL Press.

Katz, C. (1993) 'Growing girls/ closing circles.' In C. Katz and J. Monk (eds) *Full Circles: Geographies of Women over the Life Course.* London: Routledge.

Kaplan, M.M. (1992) *Mothers' Images of Motherhood.* London: Routledge.

Kitzinger, J. (1994) 'The methodology of focus groups: the importance of interaction between research participants.' *Sociology of Health and Illness 16*, 1, 103–120.

Kohn, M. (1969) *Class and conformity.* Homewood, Ill: Dorsey Press.

Kosonen, M. (1996) 'Siblings as providers of support and care during middle childhood: children's perceptions.' *Children & Society 10*, 4, 267–279.

Kruk, E. (1993) *Divorce and Disengagement.* Halifax, Nova Scotia: Fernwood.

Kumar, V. (1993) *Poverty and Inequality in the UK: The Effects on Children.* London: National Children's Bureau.

Lamb, M. (1987) *The Father's Role: Cross-national Perspectives.* Hillsdale, NJ: Laurence Erlbaum.

Lasch, C. (1977) *Haven in a Heartless World.* New York: Basic Books.

Laybourn, A. (1986) 'Traditional strict working class parenting – an undervalued system.' *British Journal of Social Work 16*, 6, 625–44.

Laybourn, A. (1994) *The Only Child.* Edinburgh: HMSO.

Laybourn, A., Brown, J. and Hill, M. (1996) *Hurting on the Inside: Children, Families and Alcohol.* Aldershot: Avebury.

LeFrancois, G. (1990) *The Lifespan.* New York: Wadsworth.

Levin, I. (1995) 'Children's perception of their family.' *Annale dell'Istituto di Dirritto e Procedura penale,* 55–74.

Lewis, A. (1995) *Children's Understanding of Disability.* London: Routledge.

Lewis, C. (1995) 'In conclusion: what opportunities are open to fathers?' In P. Moss (ed) *Father Figures.* Edinburgh: HMSO.

Lewis, C. and O'Brien, M. (eds) (1987) *Reassessing Fatherhood.* London: Sage.

Lindon, J. (1996) *Growing Up: From Eight Years to Young Adulthood.* London: National Children's Bureau.

Long, G. (1995) 'Family poverty and the role of family support work.' In M. Hill, R. Hawthorne Kirk, and D. Part (eds) *Supporting Families.* Edinburgh: HMSO.

Loughran, N. (1995) 'A review of the literature.' In S. Asquith, M. Buist, N. Loughran, M. Montgomery and C. McCauley 'Children, Young People and Offending in Scotland.' Report to Scottish Office, Edinburgh.

MacIntyre, S., MacIver, S. and Soomans, A. (1993) 'Area, class and health: should we be focusing on places or people?' *Journal of Social Policy 22*, 2, 213–23.

McGurk, H. (ed.) (1992) *Childhood Social Development.* Hove: Lawrence Erlbaum.

McNeish, D. and Roberts, H. (1995) *Playing it Safe: Today's Children at Play.* London: Barnardos.

McNeish, D. (1996) 'Young people, crime, justice and punishment.' In H. Roberts and D. Sachdev (eds) *Young People's Social Attitudes. Having Their Say – The Views of Twelve–Nine Year Olds.* Bartingside: Barnardos.

Maccoby, E.E. and Martin, J.A. (1983) 'Socialisation in the context of the family: parent–child interaction.' In E.M. Hetherington (ed) *Handbook of Child Psychology: Socialisation, Personality and Social Development* vol. 4. New York: Wiley.

Marshall, K. (1997) *Children's Rights in the Balance: The Participation-Protection Debate.* Edinburgh: Stationery Office.

Matthews, M.H. (1992) *Making Sense of Place.* Hemel Hempstead: Harvester Wheatsheaf.

Mayall, B. (1993) 'Keeping healthy at home and school: "It's my body, so it's my job".' *Sociology of Health and Illness 15*, 4, 464–87.

Mayall, B. (1994a) 'Children in action at home and school.' In B. Mayall (ed) *Children's Childhoods: Observed and Experienced.* London: Falmer Press.

Mayall, B. (1994b) *Negotiating Health: Primary School Children at Home and School.* London: Cassell.

Meadows, S. (1990) *The Child as Thinker.* London: Routledge.

Melton, G. (1994) 'Is there a place for children in the new World Order?' In S. Asquith and M. Hill (eds) (1994) *Justice for Children.* Dordrecht: Martinus Nijhoff.

Middleton, S., Ashworth, K. and Walker, R. (eds) (1994) *Family Fortunes: Pressures on Parents and Children in the 1990s.* London: Children's Poverty Action Group.

Miles, S. (1996) 'Use and Consumption in the Construction of Identities'. Paper given at *British Youth Research: The New Agenda*, 26–28 January, Glasgow.

Miller, J.B. (1993) 'Learning from early relationship experience.' In S. Duck (ed) *Learning about Relationships.* London: Sage.

Modood, T., Beishon, S. and Virdee, S. (1994) *Changing Ethnic Identities.* London: Policy Studies Institute.

Moore, R.C. (1986) *Children's Domain: Play and Place in Child Development.* London: Croom Helm.

Moore, M., Sixsmith, J. and Knowles, K. (1996) *Children's Reflections on Family Life.* London: Falmer Press.

Moran, E., Warden, D., MacLeod, L., Mayes, G. and Gillies, J. (1997) 'Stranger-danger: what do children know?' *Child Abuse Review 6*, 11–23.

Morgan, D.L. (ed.) (1993) *Successful Focus Groups.* London: Sage.

Morrow, V. and Richards, M. (1996) 'The ethics of social research with children: an overview.' *Children & Society 10*, 2, 90–105.

Morss, J.R. (1996) *Growing Critical: Alternatives to Developmental Psychology.* London: Routledge.

Moss, P. (ed) (1995) *Father Figures.* Edinburgh: HMSO.

Murray, J.P. (1993) 'The developing child in a multi-media society.' In G.L. Berry and J.K. Asamen (eds) *Children & Television.* Newbury Park: Sage.

NCH Action for Children (1997) *Family Forum Findings.* London: NCH Action for Children.

Naylor, H. (1986) 'Outdoor play and play equipment.' In P. Smith (ed) *Children's Play.* London: Gordon and Breach.

Nettleton, S. and Bunton, R. (1995) 'Sociological critiques of health promotion.' In R. Bunton, S. Nettleton and R. Burrows (eds) *The Sociology of Health Promotion.* London: Routledge.

Newell, P (1993) 'The child's right to physical integrity.' *International Journal of Children's Rights, 1*,1, 101–104.

Newman, J.L., Roberts, L.R. and Syre, C.R. (1993) 'Concepts of family among children and adolescents: effect of cognitive level, gender and family structure.' *Developmental Psychology 29*, 6, 951–62.

Newson, J. and Newson, E. (1963) *Patterns of Infant Care.* Harmondsworth: Penguin.

Newson, J. and Newson, E. (1970a) *Four Years Old in an Urban Community.*Harmondsworth: Penguin.

Newson, J. and Newson, E. (1970b) 'Concepts of parenthood.' in K. Elliott (ed.) *The Family and its Future.* London: CIBA.

Newson, J. and Newson, E. (1976) *Seven Years Old in an Urban Community.* London: Allen and Unwin.

Noller, P. and Callan, V. (1991) *The Adolescent in the Family.* London: Routledge.

Nsamenang, A.B. (1992) *Human Development in Cultural Perspective.* London: Sage.

O'Brien, M., Alldred, P. and Jones, D. (1996) 'Children's constructions of family and kinship.' In J. Brannen and M. O'Brien (eds) *Children in Families*. London: Falmer Press.

Ochiltree, G. (1990) *Children in Stepfamilies*. Englewood Cliffs: Prentice Hall.

Oldman, D. (1994) 'Childhood as a mode of production.' In B. Mayall (ed) *Children's Childhoods Observed and Experienced*. London: Falmer Press.

Olweus, D. (1991) 'Bully/victim problems among school children: basic facts and effects of a school-based intervention program.' In D. Pepler and K. Rubin (eds) *The Development and Treatment of Childhood Aggression*. London: Lawrence Erlbaum Associates.

Opie, I. (1993) *The People in the Playground*. Oxford: Oxford University Press.

Opie, I. and Opie, P. (1969) *Children's Games in Street and Playground*. Oxford: Clarendon Press.

Parke, R.D. (1989) 'Social development in infancy: a 25-year perspective.' In H.W. Reese (ed) *Advances in Child Development and Behaviour*. San Diego: Academic Press.

Parker, R., Ward, H., Jackson, S., Aldgate, J. and Wedge, P. (eds) (1991) *Looking After Children: Assessing Outcomes in Child Care*. London: HMSO.

Parkinson, L. (1987) *Separation, Divorce and Families*. London: Macmillan.

Parton, N. (1991) *Governing the Family*. London: Macmillan.

Phoenix, A. and Woollett, A. (eds) (1991) *Motherhood: Meanings, Practices and Ideologies*. London: Sage.

Pringle, M.K. (1980) *The Needs of Children*. London: Hutchinson.

Pugh, G., De'Ath, E. and Smith C. (1995) *Confident Parents, Confident Children*. London: National Children's Bureau.

Qvortrup, J. (1994) 'Childhood matters: an introduction.' In J. Qvortrup, M. Bardy, G. Sgritta and H. Wintersberger (eds) *Childhood Matters*. Aldershot: Avebury.

Qvortrup, J., Bardy, M., Sgritta, G. and Wintersberger, H. (eds) (1994) *Childhood Matters*. Aldershot: Avebury.

Roche, J. and Tucker, S. (eds) (1997) *Youth in Society*. London: Sage.

Rashid, S. (1996) 'Attachment reviewed through a cultural lens.' In D. Howe (ed) *Attachment Theory and Child and Family Social Work*. Aldershot: Avebury.

Richards, M. (1995) 'Changing families.' In M. Hill, R. Kirk and D. Part (eds) *Supporting Families*. Edinburgh: HMSO.

Roberts, H. and MacDonald, G. (1998) 'Working with families in the early years.' In M. Hill (ed) *Effective Ways of Working with Families*. London: Jessica Kingsley Publishers.

Roberts, H., Smith, S.J. and Bryce, C. (1995) *Children at Risk? Safety as a Social Value*. Milton Keynes: Open University Press.

Rutter, M. and Rutter, M. (1993) *Developing Minds*. Harmondsworth: Penguin.

Sameroff, A.J. (1975) 'Transactional models in early social development.' *Human Development, 18*, 65–79.

Savin-Williams, R.C. and Berndt, T.C. (1990) 'Friendship and peer relations.' In S.E. Feldman and G.R. Elliott (eds) *At the Threshold*. Cambridge, Mass: Harvard University Press.

Schaffer, H.R. (1990) *Making Decisions about Children*. Oxford: Blackwell.

Scraton, P. (1997) *Childhood in Crisis*. London: UCL Press.

Segal, L. (1995) 'A feminist looks at the family.' In J. Muncie, M. Wetherell, R. Dallos and A. Cochrange (eds) *Understanding the Family*. London: Sage.

Sex Education Forum (1994) *Developing and Reviewing a School Sex Education Policy: A Positive Strategy*. London: National Children's Bureau.

Shamgar-Handelman, L. (1994) 'To whom does childhood belong?' In J. Qvortrup, M. Bardy, M. Sgritta and H. Wintersberger, *Childhood Matters*. Aldershot: Avebury.

Sharpe, S., Mauthner, M. and France-Dawson, M. (1996) *Family Health: A Literature Review*. London: Health Education Authority.

Silverman, W.K. La Greca, A.M. and Wasserstein, S. (1995) 'What do children worry about? Worry and their relation to anxieties.' *Child Development 66*, 671–86.

Sinclair, R. (1996) 'Children's and young people's participation in decision-making: the legal framework in social services and education.' In M. Hill and J. Aldgate (eds) *Child Welfare Services.* London: Jessica Kingsley Publishers.

Sluckin, A. (1981) *Growing up in the Playground.* London: Routledge & Kegan Paul.

Smart, C. (1997) 'Wishful thinking and harmful tinkering? Sociological reflections on family policy.' *Journal of Social Policy 26*, 3, 301–21.

Smith, P.K. (ed) (1991) *The Psychology of Grandparenthood.* London: Routledge.

Smith, P.K. and Cowie, H. (1991) *Understanding Children's Development.* Oxford: Blackwell.

Smith, P.K. and Sharp, S. (eds) (1994) *School Bullying: Insights and Perspectives.* London: Routledge.

Smith, R.S. (1997) 'Parent education: empowerment of control.' *Children & Society 11*, 108–16.

Solberg, A. (1990) 'Negotiating childhood: changing reconstructions of age for Norwegian children.' In A. James and A. Prout (eds) *Constructing and Reconstructing Childhood.* London: Falmer Press.

Sommer, D. (1998) 'The reconstruction of childhood.' *European Journal of Social Work 1*, 2.

Stolz, L.M. (1967) *Influences on Parent Behaviour.* London: Tavistock.

Sweeting, H. and West, P. (1996) *The Health of Eleven Year Olds in the West of Scotland.* Glasgow: Medical Research Council.

Terwogt, M.M. and Harris, P.J. (1993) 'Understanding of emotion.' In M. Bennet (ed) *The Child as Psychologist.* Hemel Hempstead: Harvester Wheatsheaf.

Tisdall, E.K.M. (1997) *Children Scotland Act 1995.* Edinburgh: HMSO.

Townsend, P., Davidson, N. and Whitehead, M. (1992) *The Health Divide.* Harmondsworth: Penguin.

Wade, B. and Moore, M. (1993) *Experiencing Special Education. What Young People with Special Educational Needs can Tell Us.* Buckingham: Open University Press.

Waldrop, M.F. and Halverson, C.S. (1975) 'Intensive and extensive peer behaviour: longitudinal and cross-sectional analysis.' *Child Development 46*, 19–26.

Ward, C. (1978) *The Child in the City.* London: Architectural Press.

Ward, C. (1994) 'Opportunities for childhoods in late twentieth century Britain.' In B. Mayall (ed) *Children's Childhoods Observed and Experienced.* London: Falmer Press.

Ward, H. (1995) *Looking After Children: Research into Practice.* London: HMSO.

West, P. and Sweeting, H. (1992) *Distribution of Basic Information from the 1990 Follow-up of the Twenty-07 Study Youth Cohort.* Glasgow: MRC Medical Sociology Unit.

Wetherell, M. (1995) 'Social structure, ideology and family dynamics: the case of parenting.' In J. Muncie *et al.* (eds) *Understanding the Family.* London: Sage.

White, D. and Woollett, A. (1992) *Families: A Context for Development.* London: Falmer Press.

Whitney, I. and Smith, P.K. (1993) 'A survey of the nature and extent of bullying in junior/middle and secondary schools.' *Educational Research 35*, 1, 3–25.

Williams, T., Wetton, N. and Moon, A. (1989) *A Way In.* Southampton: Health Education Authority/University of Southampton.

Willis, P. with Jones, S., Cannan, J. and Hurd, G. (1990) *Common Culture. Symbolic Work at Play in the Everyday Cultures of the Young.* Milton Keynes: Open University Press.

Wober, M. and Gunter, B. (1988) *Television and Social Control.* Aldershot: Avebury.

Woodhead, M. (1997) 'Post-script: beyond children's needs.' In A. James and A. Prout *Constructing and Reconstructing Childhood* (2nd edition). London: Falmer Press.

Woodhead, M., Light, P. and Carr, R. (eds) (1991) *Growing up in a Changing Society.* London: Routledge.

Subject Index

Author Index